The New Testament Basis
of
PACIFISM
AND
The Relevance of
an Impossible Ideal

By

G. H. C. MACGREGOR, D.D., D.Litt.

Professor of Divinity and Biblical Criticism
in the University of Glasgow

1954

FELLOWSHIP PUBLICATIONS

Box 271, Nyack, New York

THE NEW TESTAMENT BASIS OF PACIFISM

First published 1936
New and revised edition 1954

THE RELEVANCE OF AN IMPOSSIBLE IDEAL
First published 1941

New impression 1960
New impression 1966
New impression 1968
New impression 1970

Library of Congress Catalog Card Number: 60-7634

COMPOSITION BY THE BLACKFRIARS PRESS LTD., LEICESTER, ENGLAND.
PRINTED BY PHOTO-OFFSET AND MANUFACTURED IN THE UNITED STATES
OF AMERICA BY SOWERS PRINTING CO., LEBANON, PENNA.

CONTENTS

THE NEW TESTAMENT BASIS OF PACIFISM

THE RELEVANCE OF AN IMPOSSIBLE IDEAL

PREFACE TO FIRST EDITION

THIS is not a book on the practical issues involved in the problem of Peace and War. It is possible today to advocate Pacifism on any number of grounds ; for all sensible people now realize that modern war on a large scale has become a weapon far more dangerous than any of the evils from which it is supposed to defend us. But for the Christian war is primarily a moral problem, and every moral problem is ultimately theological. For this reason it is greatly to be desired that an adequate study might be made of the theological basis of Pacifism. It is not the aim of the present volume to do this, though the fringe of the subject is touched in Chapters V and VI. Much less is it our main object to argue why and how Christian Pacifism might well prove to be practical politics in the present situation. All these problems can be intelligently discussed from the Christian standpoint only when we have first asked, What, as a matter of fact, does Jesus Himself teach ? What is the bearing of New Testament doctrine as a whole on this particular question of war ? Pacifists are perhaps too apt to assume without sufficient proof that Jesus' ethic is incontestably "pacifist", and that, even if so proved, He intended the pacifist ethic to be applied to the wider sphere of social and national politics. Our opponents still more light-heartedly deny this, with an even greater lack of demonstration. This little book is offered in the hope that it will provide all Christians who are sincere workers for peace— whether they be "Pacifists" or not—with the material necessary for thinking through for themselves this greatest of all modern ethical problems.

G. H. C. MACGREGOR

Glasgow,
September, 1936

PREFACE TO NEW EDITION

IT is now sixteen years since the publication of the first edition of this book. In the interval it has enjoyed a considerable circulation on both sides of the Atlantic, and apparently it is still found to be of some value in the great debate. Accordingly, on the invitation of the Fellowship of Reconciliation, this new edition has been prepared. The world of 1952 is a very different place from that of 1936. But the message of the New Testament, like the Lord and Master whom it reveals, is "the same yesterday and today and for ever". I have therefore not found much in the book that I should wish to alter. But the final chapter has been rewritten in order to place the argument in its contemporary setting, and to deal with the latest defences of Christian non-pacifism as erected by theologians of the school of Reinhold Niebuhr. Once again the book is offered with the prayer that it may continue to be useful in the cause of peace.

G. H. C. MACGREGOR

Glasgow,
  September, 1952

THE NEW TESTAMENT BASIS OF PACIFISM

CHAPTER ONE

THE PROBLEM

IT is greatly to be desired that some other word than "Pacifism" might be discovered to describe the faith which includes among the first principles of its creed the total renunciation of war. In the popular mind "Pacifism" is equivalent to "passivism", and the consequences of not resorting to war are readily made to appear intolerable, because it is habitually assumed that the only alternative to going to war is *doing nothing*. But, whatever be true of other brands of Pacifism, that is not the *Christian* Pacifist position. For the Christian Pacifist the *negative* prohibition, which he places upon war, has its source in the *positive* imperative of the Christian ethic, which demands that every valid means must be used to set wrongs right and build human relations on a new foundation, and yet forbids the use of such means as will by their very nature stultify the end in view. It follows that the Christian Pacifist position must be based, (*a*) *not* on the repudiation of all use of force in the dealings of man with man either as individuals or as units in the community ; yet it is almost universally assumed that such a repudiation *is* the Pacifist position, and once the absurdity of that position is proved— often an easy enough task—the question is considered settled. *Nor* (*b*) is our position based on a literalistic interpretation of either the Sixth Commandment or certain sayings of Jesus in the Sermon on the Mount, though due weight must, of course, be given to those sayings in the context of Jesus' whole teaching. Even the Devil can quote Scripture, and to cite isolated passages wrested from their context is to use a boomerang which is apt to recoil on the head of the user. Rather must our position be based (*c*) on certain essential *basic principles* of the Christian ethic as set forth in Jesus' teaching and illustrated by His example. What these principles are is the question now at issue. But, subject to confirmation by our study, the following postulates may be provisionally stated for an adequate treatment of our subject.

(1) The first principle of Jesus' ethic is love towards one's neighbour.[1]

---

[1] In the broad sense in which Jesus uses the word in e.g. Luke x. 29 ff. Matt. vii. 12 further defines this principle.

(2) This ethic is in turn based upon belief in a Father God who loves all men impartially and sets an infinite value on every individual human soul.[1]

(3) All the teaching of Jesus must be interpreted in the light of His own way of life, and above all of the Cross by which His teaching was sealed.

The issue before us is therefore best framed, not by asking, Does the New Testament ethic ever allow the use of force in the resisting and conquering of evil ? So to pose the question is to invite that unfortunate confusion of "Pacifism" with "passivism". We shall rather ask, What is the specifically Christian way of meeting and overcoming evil, as set forth in the teaching, example and Cross of Jesus Christ ? Can war under any circumstances be held to be consistent with that way ? When the question is thus stated, and our three postulates are kept in view, it becomes evident that, in order to find a place for war within the New Testament ethic, it is not enough to prove that Jesus recognizes the place of law in an ordered society, that He permits a moral use of force to uphold justice, that He might even allow the use of a "sword" in self-defence against bandits. This may all be true ; and yet war, as we have come to know it, may so violate Jesus' essential principles, and so stultify the specifically Christian method of meeting evil, that its one certain issue will not be justice but moral and spiritual death. In a word, the Christian Pacifist position must rest in the main on a discrimination, in the light of the teaching and example of Jesus, between moral and non-moral uses of force, and on the affirmation that when called to the bar of the New Testament ethic, whatever may be said of certain exercises of force, war at least is seen to be under a final prohibition.

It should be hardly necessary to insist that, inasmuch as our problem is one not of political expediency but of moral obligation, the final court of appeal is the New Testament. Yet, as concerns this particular problem, the average Christian is still in such bondage to the traditional dogma of Church and State, so painfully evolved by orthodox Protestant theology,[2] that one feels a good deal of sympathy with the outburst of G. J. Heering : "If the pure and exalted ethic of the Gospel is to come into its rights, it will have to hold dogmatics at arm's length for the present, to prevent the latter from paralysing it before it has been able to display its power and aim."[3] The purpose of the following pages is to allow the authentic accents of the New Testament to be heard.

[1] Matt. v. 45 ; x. 29–31 ; xvi. 26.
[2] For this see Chapter Seven.
[3] G. J. Heering, *The Fall of Christianity*, p. 10.

One would have hoped that, whatever our difference of opinion as to the validity and practicability under modern conditions of Jesus' teaching, it would at least be possible to reach agreement as to what the teaching actually is, even in its bearing upon so complex a problem as that of Peace and War. Yet the most sincere Christians still find themselves poles apart in their interpretation of the evidence. Few will deny that war *as an instrument of national policy* (the qualification is often important) is a complete denial of the teaching, spirit and methods of Jesus. But there agreement ends, and generally speaking Christians may be grouped according as they hold one of three views.

(1) Firstly it is urged that the teaching and example of Jesus are essentially "pacifist" and reveal, above all in the Cross, an alternative method of meeting and overcoming evil which renders all violent methods obsolete. War as we know it today, involving as it does an utter prostitution both of moral values and of the Christian conception of personal relationships, cannot under any conditions be brought within the orbit of the Christian ethic. The Church, if she is to be true to her function as the Body of Christ and His organ in society, is under all circumstances bound by that ethic, however impracticable it may appear when judged by considerations of prudence, expediency and probable result : "The foolishness of God is wiser than men ; and the weakness of God is stronger than men."[1] This is the Christian Pacifist position and admits of no ambiguity.

(2) Many equally sincere Christians, among them, it must be admitted, not a few eminent dogmatic theologians, argue on the contrary that the teaching of Jesus is *not* necessarily "pacifist". Pacifism indeed appears as a dangerous modern "heresy". The New Testament ethic is based on the law of righteousness as well as on the law of love, and the besetting sin of Pacifism is to exalt love at the expense of righteousness. The Law is the basis of the Gospel, and even in the New Testament it remains not merely as so much scaffolding, to be scrapped (as is done, it is alleged, by the Pacifist) when its purpose is served, but as an integral part of the completed building. There are elements in both the teaching and the example of Jesus which suggest that He would approve the violent application of force in restraint of evil, and once this is admitted the line cannot be drawn even at war. The Pacifist's absolute prohibition of war rests upon a basis which is sentimental rather than ethical, and can find no support in the New Testament, which nowhere forbids the taking up of arms in a just cause. In all of which there is much truth, of which the Pacifist does well to be reminded. But is the scope of Law adequately delimited, or its final sublimation and

[1] 1 Cor. i. 25.

"fulfilment" in the Gospel sufficiently realized ? These particular questions will be fully dealt with in Chapter Six.

(3) It is possible, finally, to take a middle position : Jesus' teaching, if taken at its face value and consistently applied, with due weight given to that which is distinctively His own in His method of dealing with evil, undeniably implies what today would be called the "pacifist" attitude. But Jesus' ethical teaching, as we have it briefly reported in the Gospels, cannot be held to cover the whole field of moral obligation with which mankind is confronted today. Conditions have arisen in State and Society which were not before the mind of Jesus, who was legislating for an ideal "kingdom", and not for the imperfect world in which we live. In such a world situations are bound to arise in which the use of the war method is the lesser of two evils, even if it conflicts with Jesus' method. The Christian's duty as a citizen justifies him in refusing to take literally an ethic which he might feel constrained to obey if the Kingdom of Heaven had come on earth. According to this third point of view the debate should not be concerning any ambiguity in Jesus' teaching, which is admitted to be unequivocally pacifist, but rather concerning its comprehensiveness, its practicability, the point at which for the Church it becomes fully applicable in our slow progress towards a completely Christian social and international order. The ethic of the Sermon on the Mount must be acknowledged to be unambiguous : but meantime circumstances compel us to declare a "moratorium" upon it.

It is perhaps not entirely without significance that, over against the purely dogmatic theologians, with their possibly exaggerated deference to traditional Church dogma, this is the position adopted by several eminent New Testament scholars who are not themselves Pacifists. Professor H. Windisch, one of the foremost modern continental New Testament scholars, will serve as an example : "Condemnation of all forms of war is the only attitude congenial with the spirit of the Sermon on the Mount."[1] "The critic must concede to the objector to military service that his exegesis is the more accurate. He cannot defend himself against Tolstoyan practice by any dogmatic exegesis."[2] Windisch further quotes with full approval the opinion of Professor Baumgarten, which is all the more impressive as both are non-Pacifists writing during the First World War : "Not only the war of aggression but also defensive warfare is ruled out by the Sermon on the Mount. . . . We have primarily to recognize, however hard it may be at present (1915) to do so, that the waging of war has no place in the moral and spiritual teaching of Jesus."[3]

[1] *Der Sinn der Bergpredigt*, 1929, p. 150.
[2] *Theol. Rundschau*, 1915, p. 288.
[3] Ibid., pp. 338, 348.

Similarly Harnack : "It requires no further proof to establish firmly that the Gospel excludes all violence, and has nothing in common with war, nor will permit it."[1] Yet Harnack vigorously defends participation in war by Christians ! In a word, the view of such scholars is that the ethic of Jesus is indisputably pacifist, but it is not comprehensive enough to be applicable to the affairs of the modern state and nation. While acknowledging the scientific honesty of such a position, which is greatly to be preferred to that of the apologist who seeks to discover loopholes through which war may actually be brought within the pale of Christian ethics, we shall have to ask whether such a compromise either does justice to the New Testament imperative, or can permanently satisfy the enlightened Christian conscience.

---

[1] *Militia Christi*, p. 2. I am indebted for these quotations to G. J. Heering, *The Fall of Christianity*, pp. 31, 35, 63, 64.

CHAPTER TWO

DOES THE NEW TESTAMENT SANCTION WAR?

BOTH sides to the present controversy must plead guilty to the unfortunate practice of quoting isolated texts, often wrested from their context ; and in view of the constant and light-hearted misapplication of certain well-known passages, it will be well to deal with them, before entering upon a more positive and constructive study of the New Testament evidence. The passages will first be quoted from the Revised Version ; the use made of them by certain apologists for militarism will then be indicated, and, where necessary, a corrective will be provided. We shall confine ourselves to the New Testament. Admittedly much use is made in certain quarters of passages drawn from the more war-like sections of the Old Testament ; the question whether the will and the hand of God are to be traced in the aggressive wars of Israel is one that must be frankly faced.[1] But our present task is not the philosophy of history but the interpretation of Scripture, and if the New Testament is always to be understood in the light of the Old, rather than the Old Testament re-interpreted in the light of the New, then we may well despair of any progress towards the truth. "For the man who relates the question of Christianity and War to the whole Bible, while regarding the Bible as a unity, the whole of which lies on one level, the problem is insoluble. But he for whom the Scriptures are not a static unity, but an organic (for an organism passes through phases of growth), a progressive and ever fuller revelation of God's being and will, *he* will be able to see an ascending line, which finds its goal and zenith in Jesus Christ."[2] Moreover it often seems to be forgotten that Jesus prefaces the most crucial of all our passages with the words, "Ye have heard that it was said by them of old time . . . But I say unto you . . ."[3] Could Jesus have possibly indicated more clearly that He claimed, and was indeed exercising, the right to correct the misconceptions even of the Old Testament Scriptures themselves ? As Windisch again well says : "The brutal dictates of War and State in the Old Testament simply do not arise for the man who has grasped the antitheses of the Sermon on the Mount."[4]

[1] This subject is touched upon in Chapter Five.
[2] Heering, *The Fall of Christianity*, p. 19.
[3] Matt. v. 21, 27, 33, 38, 43.
[4] *Der Sinn der Bergpredigt*, 1929, p. 154.

THE CLEANSING OF THE TEMPLE[1] : especially John ii. 15, "**And he made a scourge of cords, and cast all out of the temple, both the sheep and the oxen.**" Jesus, it is argued, was no pusillanimous Pacifist, but a man capable of righteous anger, which expressed itself in an act of aggressive personal violence against the desecrators of the Temple. What better justification does a Christian need even for aggressive warfare in a just cause ?

This scene admittedly indicates a reaction against evil on the part of Jesus much more strenuous than the meek acquiescence which is commonly misrepresented as Pacifism. But we are not concerned to deny that there is room in Jesus' ethic for a discriminating use of force. Note, however, the following points :

(1) It is the Fourth Gospel alone which mentions the "scourge". Jewish tradition held that the Messiah at his coming would bear a lash for the chastisement of evil-doers (cf. the "fan" in Matt. iii. 12). Scholars are agreed that the whole significance of the scene in this Gospel is Messianic, and the Evangelist's well-known love of symbolism suggests that the "scourge" is to be regarded as an emblem of authority rather than as a weapon of offence. But even if the word is to be taken literally, a correct rendering of the Greek makes it clear that the whip was used only on the animals.[2] Finally, the word[3] which in its English dress "cast out" gives the impression of extreme violence, is frequently used in the New Testament without any such suggestion, e.g. "Pray ye therefore the Lord of the harvest, that he *send forth* labourers into his harvest."[4] The parallel verse in Mark might quite legitimately be translated without any hint of exceptional violence : "He entered into the temple, and began· to *send out* them that sold and them that bought in the temple."[5]

---

[1] Mark xi. 15–18 ; Matt. xxi. 12–13 ; Luke xix. 45–6 ; John ii. 13–17.

[2] The Greek here is : πάντας ἐξέβαλεν ἐκ τοῦ ἱεροῦ, τά τε πρόβατα καὶ τοὺς βόας.

Note (a) a common and correct use of the particles τε . . . καί is to subdivide a subject or object, previously mentioned, into its component parts. Here "πάντας" "all of them" (i.e. all the animals), is further defined as consisting of "sheep" (πρόβατα) and "oxen" (βόας). Cf. Matt. xxii. 10 : πάντας οὓς εὗρον, πονηρούς τε καὶ ἀγαθούς. Another good example is Rom. ii. 9–10, where the construction occurs twice. Cf. also Luke xxii. 66.

(b) It is sometimes objected that, if πάντας referred only to the animals, it should naturally be in the neuter gender agreeing with πρόβατα (the nearest word), rather than the masculine agreeing with βόας; ; being masculine it must refer to the men. But the grammatical rule is that, when one adjective qualifies two nouns of different genders, it will agree with the masculine or feminine noun rather than with the neuter noun, irrespective of position. A good example is Heb. iii. 6 : ἐὰν τὴν παρρησίαν καὶ τὸ καύχημα τῆς ἐλπίδος μέχρι τέλους βεβαίαν κατάσχωμεν.

[3] ἐκβάλλειν

[4] Matt. ix. 38.

[5] Mark xi. 15.

B

(2) Had Jesus used violence, He must inevitably have provoked retaliation and been overpowered by superior numbers. Much more probably it was the compelling "authority" of His words which overawed His opponents ; their conscience condemned them, and they withdrew in disorder. Moral authority, unarmed, triumphed where violence would have been futile. There would seem to be an argument here for Pacifism at least equal to that against it.

(3) In any case the passage has no relevance whatever to war. "My house", says Jesus, "shall be called a house of prayer *for all the nations*, but ye have made it a den of robbers."[1] Probably the scene of the desecration was the outer Court, which was open to Gentiles. The foreigner was being robbed of his right of approach to Israel's God. An incident which is so often adduced as an apology for war can in fact be read as a protest by Jesus on behalf of international goodwill.

THE CENTURION AT CAPERNAUM[2] : **" Jesus marvelled and said to them that followed, Verily I say unto you, I have not found so great faith, no, not in Israel."** It is pointed out that Jesus commends the centurion, and never hints that there is anything wrong in the occupation of a soldier, or that the centurion should give up the profession of arms. Jesus, then, would give no countenance to Pacifism. A similar use is made of Luke iii. 14 ff., where John the Baptist answers the soldiers' questions without condemning their calling. Thus Augustine, quoted by Calvin with approval : "If Christian discipline condemned all wars, when the soldiers asked counsel as to the way of salvation, they would have been told to cast away their arms. . . . Those whom he orders to be contented with their pay, he certainly does not forbid to serve."[3] In reply we may note :

(1) It was the centurion's faith, not his calling, which Jesus commended. Moreover this is one of the very few occasions on which Jesus is said to have "marvelled". The chief impression left by the story is that Jesus was greatly surprised to find faith in so unlikely a quarter, though doubtless this was chiefly because the man was a heathen.

(2) An "argument from silence" is always precarious, and never more so than when applied to the Gospels. Modern scholarship is insisting more and more that only an exceedingly limited number

[1]Mark xi. 17.
[2]Matt. viii. 5–10 ; Luke vii. 1–10.
[3]There is a certain unconscious humour in the fact that in the *Westminster Confession*, Chapter XXIII, the first New Testament authority cited in support of the proposition that "Christians . . . may lawfully, now under the New Testament, wage war upon just and necessary occasions" is Luke iii. 14 : "And soldiers also asked him saying, And we, what must we do? And he said unto them, *Do violence to nó man . . .*"

of motives has determined the selection of material which has found a place in the earliest collections. Even sayings of Jesus would tend to be excluded, if they appeared irrelevant to the main end in view, however useful they might prove today for the solution of our modern problems. That end was the proclamation of the Christian Gospel of salvation. As Dr. Martin Dibelius says, "The first Christians had no interest in reporting the life and passion of Jesus objectively to mankind. . . . They wanted nothing else than to win as many as possible to salvation in the last hour just before the end of the world, which they believed to be at hand. This salvation had been revealed in Jesus, and any morsel of information about Jesus was full of meaning for them *only when it pertained to salvation*." "The aim of the Gospels is to furnish proof of the message of salvation which has been preached."[1] Moreover, the story of the centurion belongs to a group of what have been called "Pronouncement Stories", whose "chief characteristic . . . is that they culminate in a saying of Jesus which expresses some ethical or religious precept".[2] In other words the interest of such stories is focused upon one particular motif, in this case upon the centurion's faith and Jesus' response to it. We have no right, therefore, to expect to find in it an estimate by Jesus, either favourable or otherwise, of the supplicant's military calling, nor to deduce anything from His silence. In the same chapter in Luke[3] Jesus commends "a woman in the city, which was a sinner", but He is not supposed to condone her prostitution because He is silent about it. He commends Zacchaeus the tax-collector[4] without referring to his profession : must He be held therefore to condone "graft" ? The New Testament contains no word of protest against slavery : are we to conclude, therefore, that slavery is in accordance with the Christian ethic, and that those who led the protest against it were perverting the Gospel ?

(3) The question of war hardly arises here. The Roman soldiery in Palestine corresponded rather to a police-force ; and Jesus could not have publicly condemned such service, even had He desired to do so, without coming into premature conflict with Rome, and ultimately identifying Himself with violent revolt, to the stultification of His own pacifist ethic. There is much about which both Jesus and the early Church were silent because of their eager expectation of the "Kingdom's" imminent coming, which would render obsolete any denunciation of Rome and her ways.

(4) It should surely be obvious that one may gladly recognize splendid qualities in individual soldiers, as in all other professions,

---

[1] *Gospel Criticism and Christology*, 1935, pp. 16, 31. Italics mine.
[2] See Vincent Taylor, *The Formation of the Gospel Tradition*, pp. 63 ff.
[3] Luke vii. 36 ff.   [4] Luke xix. 9.

without thereby committing oneself to approval of their calling. It is interesting to find the militaristically minded, but honest, Harnack writing thus of the three centurions in the Gospels : "These stories are not told with a view to glorifying the soldier's profession. . . . In all these cases it is of secondary importance to the narrative that the men were soldiers. It is very true that these stories have since been exploited again and again in the interest of the profession of war."[1] And Windisch concludes a reference to our passage by re-marking : "Here again the attitude of Jesus gives no sanction to militarism."[2]

"**Think not that I came to send peace on earth : I came not to send peace, but a sword.**"[3] It is often argued from this saying that Jesus foresaw the inevitability of war under the Christian dispensation, and indeed conceived that the purpose of His mission would find its fulfilment in war rather than in peace. It is part of the presumption of Pacifism to assume that the Kingdom must be one of universal peace. But :

(1) Does this verse really express *purpose* ? More probably it is a good example of a common Semitic idiom whereby what is really a consequence, especially a tragic one, is ironically expressed as a purpose[4]. Jesus means, "I came on a mission of mercy, and the only result, alas, is a 'sword'."

(2) As a matter of fact there is no reference whatever in the verse to war. Are we seriously to picture the daughter using the "sword" upon her mother ? Instead of "sword" Luke here much more literally has "*division*" ($\delta\iota\alpha\mu\epsilon\rho\iota\sigma\mu\delta$s), the same word as in Hebrews iv. 12 : "The word of God is living, and active, and sharper than any two-edged sword, and piercing even to the *dividing* of soul and spirit." Just as the word of God is said to sift the component parts of a man's being, so will Jesus' mission sift the true from the false in human society. The context shows that the "division" in question has nothing to do with war, but refers to the misunderstanding and even persecution to be endured by the loyal Christian at the hands of those who should be his best friends. The words might find a true illustration, not in a war supposedly sanctioned by Jesus, but far more fittingly in the conscientious objector to war, ostracized by society, disowned even by his own family, on account of loyalty to Jesus' teaching as he understands it.

[1] *Militia Christi*, p. 52.
[2] *Theol. Rundschau*, 1915, p. 343.
[3] Matt. x. 34 ; cf. Luke xii. 51.
[4] A good example from the Old Testament is Hosea viii. 4 : "Of their silver and their gold have they made them idols, that they may be cut off," i.e. "with the result that they have been cut off"

"When ye shall hear of wars and rumours of wars, be not troubled : these things must needs come to pass."[1] With this saying may be compared the various prophecies of war in the Apocalypse.[2] What right, it is asked, has the Christian to renounce war, when Jesus Himself foretells that "it must needs come to pass" ? "I would very much like to know", runs a typical "letter to the Editor", "what justification writers have for their extreme pacifist views. Whether we wish it or not, we still have the Battle of Armageddon to face. Will these friends then, when the great battle of Christ's forces against anti-Christ takes place, be pacifists ?"[3] We may remark in reply :

(1) It is hardly necessary at this time of day to caution the intelligent reader against fantastically literal interpretations of the Book of Revelation. The saying of Jesus Himself, if such it is, requires much more careful consideration. But it is probable that here, too, we have a highly-coloured picture, characteristic of Jewish Apocalyptic, of the catastrophes which are to precede the end of the age. It is very doubtful whether Mark xiii, 7-8 can be considered as belonging to the authentic teaching of Jesus. Modern scholars are almost unanimous in regarding this chapter as a composite section consisting of a short independent Jewish, or Jewish-Christian, apocalypse, which has been combined with genuine sayings of Jesus. The Jewish stratum appears to consist of verses 7-8, 14-20, 24-7, which if read consecutively will be found to hang together to form an independent unit. It is in the intervening verses that we may expect to find genuine sayings of Jesus.

(2) The warning of a dire succession of wars has proved only too tragically true. But, even if we should feel compelled to accept this as an authentic saying of Jesus, it is not necessary to conclude that, contrary to the whole trend of His teaching, Jesus has laid upon His disciples the obligation to take part in such wars, which are due in part, as He Himself suggests, to the emergence of "false Christs and false prophets" who will "lead astray, if possible, even the elect."[4]

(3) As for the warlike passages in the Book of Revelation, we may allow G. J. Heering to give us a summary of his own conclusions and those of other scholars : "Christian apocalyptic was built up in the first century on the Jewish model, and largely out of Jewish materials of which the Revelation of St. John is the biblical example. Harnack writes : 'The apocalyptic eschatology preserves traces of the warlike Messiah by taking them over to its portrait of Jesus,' but 'one notices that the warlike element is wholly confined to the

[1]Mark xiii. 7, and parallels.
[2]Rev. vi. 4–8 ; xi. 7 ff. ; xii. 7 ff. ; xiii. 7 ; xvi. 16 ; xvii. 14 ; xix. 11–21.
[3]*British Weekly*, August 30th, 1934.
[4]Mark xiii. 22.

apocalyptic eschatology, and does not extend to the figure of Christ outside it.' And as the Messiah of apocalypse fights with angels at his side, and not with men, this action in no way affects the example which the Christ of the Gospels has left behind. 'Heavenly beings and superhuman heavenly powers alone wage war on God's behalf. When men fight, they are doomed to destruction ; only the devil lets men fight for him.' The author of Apocalypse is convinced of that,"[1]

"**But now, he that hath a purse, let him take it, and likewise a wallet ; and he that hath no sword, let him sell his cloke and buy one. For I say unto you, that this which is written must be fulfilled in me. And he was reckoned with transgressors : for that which concerneth me hath fulfilment. And they said, Lord, behold, here are two swords. And he said, It is enough.**"[2]

A typical comment from the anti-pacifist viewpoint is that of the German theologian Spitta during the war : "See ! Jesus has summoned His followers to armed defence ! He was no tender pacifist."[3] Is there any reply ?

(1) It must be frankly confessed that the passage is one of the most puzzling with which we have to deal, and it has always perplexed scholars, even when they have no axe to grind in connection with the present controversy. Thus Weiss writes in his famous *Commentary* : "The martial note in this word is in direct contradiction to many others which definitely forbid resistance. It is in direct opposition to the whole spirit of primitive Christianity." If Spitta's comment is justified, then it is very hard to explain Jesus' complete change of front when His disciples take Him at His word and put up an armed defence in Gethsemane: "Put up again thy sword in its place : for all they that take the sword shall perish with the sword."[4]

(2) Short of a definitely pacifist explanation, much the best interpretation is one suggested to me by my colleague, Principal W. A. Curtis : "It is evident that Jesus had not forbidden the disciples in their journey from Galilee to Jerusalem to carry weapons and that these weapons were nothing but the customary means of protection which travellers have always used *when beyond the reach of law* and armed protection. In Jerusalem they were *under the shadow of the law*, Jewish and Roman, and their arms were in abeyance. In the passage quoted the traveller's sword is like the

[1]Heering, *The Fall of Christianity*, p. 30, quoting Harnack, *Militia Christi*, p. 6, and Windisch, *Der Mess. Krieg*, p. 76.
[2]Luke xxii. 36–8.
[3]*Theol. Rundschau*, 1915, p.235 ; quoted by Heering, op. cit. p. 24.
[4]Matt. xxvi. 52.

purse, and the wallet, and the sandals, and the cloak, a symbol of homeless wandering on an urgent and dangerous mission, far more formidable than their shorter and safer errands hitherto at His bidding. It may be inferred that Jesus had taken no exception to them bearing the ordinary means of self-defence when travelling in bandit-infested country *beyond the protection of armed authority*." (Italics throughout are mine.) The point of this interpretation is the distinction drawn between Jesus' permission of arms when "beyond the reach of law", and His prohibition of them "under the shadow of the law". This is thought to explain Jesus' apparent *volte face* at the arrest. It is also assumed that Jesus envisages henceforth a more "dangerous and urgent mission", which will take the disciples to a greater extent than hitherto beyond the pale of law, and therefore justify the bearing of defensive arms. This exegesis is admittedly attractive : but there are serious difficulties :

(*a*) The command to "buy a sword" appears to be given with the prospect of Jesus' coming arrest and death definitely in view, and with the purpose of meeting some eventuality connected with this coming crisis : verse 37, "*For . . .* that which concerneth me hath fulfilment," makes this quite plain.

(*b*) Yet, if anything is certain, it is that the command cannot have been given with a view to resistance at the arrest ; Jesus' rebuke, "Put up thy sword again into its place,"[1] rules this out.

(*c*) It is difficult, again, to see how the approach of Jesus' death, or even the Crucifixion itself, should be thought of as so altering the disciples' circumstances that, whereas formerly they travelled under the protection of common law, where no "sword" was needed, they would henceforth be travelling (as this interpretation assumes) "beyond the protection of armed authority", where possession of arms might be permitted. The interpretation seems somewhat arbitrarily to read into the passage this distinction between two environments, one "under the shadow of the law" and the other "beyond the reach of the law". The distinction is, of course, a real one ; but it is doubtful whether it is implied in this passage.

(3) Many modern scholars have accordingly suspected the passage, and even the connection of verse 36 with verse 38 is questioned. The incident occurs only in Luke, and it is perhaps suggestive that in the sequel[2] this Evangelist tones down Jesus' sharp rebuke as recorded by Matthew[3] into the ambiguous words, "Suffer ye thus far." It is not a little tempting to guess that our crux is simply an awkward attempt on the part of the "Lukan editor" to prepare the way for the sequel in Gethsemane, and so to justify the disciples' attempt at violent resistance. It is significant that else-

[1]Matt. xxvi. 52.   [2]Luke xxii. 51.   [3]Matt. xxvi. 52.

where Luke tends to slur over the shortcomings of the Twelve. For example, while Mark tells frankly of the unworthy claim made by James and John to places of special honour in the Kingdom,[1] and Matthew begins the white-washing process by transferring the blame to their mother,[2] Luke tactfully omits the incident altogether.

(4) If this be considered too drastic a cutting of the knot, we are left with three alternatives. The command to "buy a sword" must be taken either :

(a) Quite literally and seriously, as the opponents of Pacifism assert. But, as J. M. Creed in our foremost commentary in English on St. Luke's Gospel puts it, "It is unlikely that Jesus seriously entertained the thought of armed resistance, which indeed would be in conflict with the whole tenor of His life and teaching."[3] Similarly F. C. Burkitt : "It is impossible to believe that the command to buy a sword was meant literally or seriously."[4] It should perhaps be remarked that neither of these scholars is a Pacifist.

(b) Seriously, but metaphorically. "It seems better", writes Dr. Creed, "to assume that Jesus intended the words of verse 36 to be accepted in a general sense as a warning that disaster is coming,[5] and that the disciples misunderstood Him."[6] Then Jesus, in despair at the denseness of His hearers who have taken him up literally and produced two swords, breaks off the conversation with the common Semitic formula, "It is enough !"[7]—as we might say, "That will do !"

(c) Literally, but ironically—the words being spoken by Jesus in what Dr. Burkitt calls a mood of "ironical foreboding". The words "it is enough" might then be taken as a semi-playful reminder to the literally-minded disciples. The absurdly inadequate "two swords" are "enough" with which to resist the might of Rome ! So far from being a summons to armed defence, Jesus' words are rather a wistful reminder of the utter futility of armed resistance.

Our conclusion then is that these words have been made to carry much greater weight than is legitimate. But it must be allowed that, so far as this context goes (if it is read apart from the sequel in Gethsemane), we cannot cite Jesus as definitely discountenancing the recognized habit of carrying arms in self-defence. But, even so, is it necessary to suppose that, where a Livingstone was content to go armed only with the Gospel of love, the Master Himself and His company, in contradiction to the whole spirit and trend of His teaching, would rely upon "swords" ?

---

[1]Mark x. 37.   [2]Matt. xx. 20.
[3]The Gospel according to St. Luke, p. 270.
[4]See The Gospel History and its Transmission, pp. 140 ff.
[5]Cf. Matt. x. 34 ; Luke xii. 51.   [6]Creed, op. cit. p. 270.
[7]See Deut. iii. 26 ; and cf. the similar phrase in Mark xiv. 41.

"**All they that take the sword shall perish with the sword.**"[1] This is quite commonly interpreted as meaning that the aggressor, no doubt, is to perish ; but how, if not by the "sword" of the defender ? It is argued that Jesus thus sanctions defensive warfare as an instrument necessary for the accomplishment of God's just and holy purpose.

But the saying can be thus misused only when it is wrested from its context by the omission of the first clause, "**Put up again thy sword in its place!**" For it is precisely the *defensive* "sword" which is here coming under condemnation. The sword, even when used in defence, will recoil upon him who uses it. There are not two "swords" in view, the unrighteous sword of the aggressor and the righteous sword of the defender. The "perishing by the sword" is inherent in the very use of the sword, not a penalty exacted by a third party. It is true that there is an echo of this saying in the warlike Book of Revelation, where it appears to be misunderstood in much the same way as it is by our militarists : "If any man shall kill with the sword, with the sword must he be killed."[2] But the words as spoken by Jesus are regularly interpreted by early Christian writers as an absolute prohibition of military service. Here, for example, is Tertullian : "Shall it be held lawful to make an occupation of the sword, when the Lord proclaims that he who uses the sword shall perish by the sword ?"[3]

"**When the strong man armed guardeth his own court, his goods are in peace**"[4]—from which it is argued that according to Jesus Himself the only true security is to be armed to the teeth. To refute such exegesis it is only necessary to read on : "**But when a stronger than he shall come upon him, and overcome him, he taketh from him his whole armour wherein he trusted, and divideth his spoils.**" If security lies in arms, then it is only when each man is stronger than all his neighbours ! The whole stress is upon the futility of "the armour wherein he trusted". In any case there is no reason to suppose that Jesus blesses war merely because He uses a simile drawn from arms. Is He to be thought to bless burglary when He compares the coming of the Son of Man with the breaking in of a thief ?[5]

"**If my kingdom were of this world, then would my servants fight.**"[6] Jesus is explaining that a Kingdom such as His is not one which is defended by force of arms, for "it is not of this world". Yet the inference has actually been wrung from the verse that conversely, when the issue *is* one of loyalty to a worldly king-

[1]Matt. xxvi. 52. [2]Rev. xiii. 10. [3]*de Corona*, xi.
[4]Luke xi. 21 f. [5]Matt. xxiv. 42 ff. [6]John xviii. 36.

dom, Jesus *would* have His servants fight. Even Luther argues from this passage that Jesus had no quarrel with war itself, provided it were waged by the Sovereign for just ends. Were Jesus a worldly Sovereign, He would do the same.

But the saying begins, **"My kingdom is NOT of this world."** One might as well argue that, if Jesus' view of His mission and purpose were the opposite of what in point of fact it is, then His ethical teaching would be likely to suffer a similar metamorphosis— which is obvious, but not very helpful ! The very essence of the New Testament challenge is surely that the Christian is to practise here in the world an ethic which is not of the world.

"But the king was wroth ; and he sent his armies, and destroyed those murderers, and burned their city."[1] Together with this verse we may consider other similar parabolic illustrations.[2]

It is sometimes argued that various allusions in Jesus' parables, for example descriptions of kings and masters inflicting severe penalties on offending subjects, must be held to imply that Jesus would approve a similar application of armed violence and other forcible social sanctions to wrongdoers in real life. A correct appreciation of the whole trend and method of Jesus' teaching will decisively negative any such suggestion. In his parabolic illustrations Jesus can be held neither to approve nor condemn the actual practices from which they are drawn. He always uses these illustrations to underline some one fundamental moral or spiritual truth. For example, Luke xvii. 7-10 has as its central thought the truth that the Christian is always on duty. It does not teach that the Christian himself may own and overwork slaves !

"Put on the whole armour of God,"[3] and numerous other Pauline military metaphors.[4] Surely, it is argued, Paul must approve of warfare, or else he would not so constantly use military metaphors to describe the Christian way of life.

Once again a study of the context is sufficient refutation. The emphasis is regularly upon the *contrast* between ordinary warfare and the Christian way of life : **"Our wrestling is NOT against flesh and blood."**[5] The Christian will fight only with the weapons of the Spirit. It would be truer to argue that Paul deliberately uses the figure of military warfare in order to stress the point that the

[1]Matt. xxii. 7.
[2]Cf. Matt. xviii. 34 f. ; xxiv. 50 f. ; xxii. 13 ; xxv. 30 ; Mark xii. 9 ; Luke xix. 27, etc.
[3]Eph. vi. 10-17.
[4]Cf. Rom. xiii. 12 ; 2 Cor. vi. 7 ; 1 Thess. v. 8 ; 1 Tim. i. 18 ; vi. 12 ; 2 Tim. ii. 3 f.
[5]Eph. vi. 12.

warfare of the Christian is something wholly different. The Christian must discover "the moral equivalent of war." It is **"the good fight of faith"** which is in question.[1] No early Christian would have dreamed of appealing to such metaphors in justification of war ; the very reverse is the truth. "I am a soldier of Christ," cried a soldier-convert martyred for refusing military service, "and may not fight ; the weapons of blood are discarded, that the weapons of peace may be girded on."[2]

"Greater love hath no man than this, that a man lay down his life for his friends."[3] War may sometimes be justified, so it is said, if only because it calls forth the supreme expression of this Christ-like love.

This argument must be dealt with more fully in Chapter Six. But meantime, we may remind ourselves :

(1) Jesus did *not* say, "that a man kills his enemies for the sake of his friends". Reverently though one acknowledges that multitudes have so laid down their lives in battle for the sake of their friends, so to do is not the aim and object of the soldier's training and profession. The soldier is trained to protect himself and to kill others, and the better soldier he is, the more successful will he be in doing both. The self-sacrifice is but an inevitable by-product of the soldier's main task, and we must not allow sentiment to blind us to that fact.

(2) An even higher expression of this Christ-like love is envisaged in the great words of Paul : "God commendeth His own love towards us, in that, while we were yet *sinners*, Christ died for us." Jesus died not only for His "friends". "When we were *enemies*, we were reconciled to God by the death of His Son."[4]

(3) The essence of this Christ-like sacrifice is that it should be wholly voluntary : "Therefore doth the Father love me, because I lay down my life. . . . No man taketh it away from me, but I lay it down of myself."[5] Though one humbly, yet proudly, agrees that thousands have died on the battlefield in such a spirit, what can there possibly be in common between such an ideal and a war-system which conscripts free human personalities to be the instrument of mass-slaughter and in the end to become themselves "cannon-fodder" ? We gain nothing by mincing words.

(4) It is easy to come perilously near to blasphemy when we thus appeal to the Cross in the name of Mars. "The Cross", says Erasmus, "is the banner and standard of Him who has overcome

---

[1] 1 Tim. vi. 12.
[2] Quoted by Heering, *The Fall of Christianity*, p. 53.
[3] John xv. 13.   [4] Rom. v. 8, 10.   [5] John x. 17 f.

and triumphed, not by fighting and slaying, but by His own bitter death. With the Cross do ye deprive of life your brother, whose life was rescued by the Cross ?"

Two other much-quoted passages should perhaps fall to be dealt with here : Mark xii. 17, "Render unto Caesar the things that are Caesar's, and unto God the things that are God's" ; and Romans xiii. 1–7, where Paul writes as if he considered the "higher powers", that is to say the "civil authority" or the "civil magistrate", to be a Divine institution to which loyal obedience is due. It will be better, however, to reserve both passages for treatment in the Chapter on "Christ and Caesar".

CHAPTER THREE

THE WAY OF JESUS IN PERSONAL RELATIONSHIPS

WHERE are we to look for that which is specifically distinctive and original in Jesus' teaching and example concerning personal relationships, particularly with reference to the meeting and overcoming of evil ? We might perhaps summarize thus : The essence of His teaching is distilled in His "Golden Rule", "All things whatsoever ye would that men should do unto you, even so do ye also unto them."[1] It is crystallized in two commandments on which He declares the whole Law to hang, complete love of God, and unfailing love of neighbour.[2] His blessing is for the peacemakers.[3] He holds it to be nearer His own spirit to suffer wrong than to inflict it, even when the suffering is undeserved.[4] Instead of seeking revenge He calls on His disciples to love their enemies and to pray for those who persecute them.[5] Not only His teaching but also His life bears witness that error must be overcome not by violence but by truth, hatred not by enmity but by love, evil not by its own weapons but by good. Finally His acceptance of the Cross was a summary in action of all that He had taught in word. And, most important of all, His ethic is founded throughout on His distinctive belief about God. The peacemakers are blessed because they are the children of God and share His nature.[6] His disciples will love even their enemies, in order that they may be "sons of their Father who is in heaven".[7] They will strive to be "perfect", because "their heavenly Father is perfect".[8] We have here morals founded on theology, an ethic of the Brotherhood of Man founded on a theology of the Fatherhood of God.

Let us follow Jesus in His application of this ethic. It is no part of our aim to argue that this specifically Christian ethic was intended by Jesus either to annul the sanction of law, or to render obsolete a civil authority capable of a moral use of force. But it does suggest that Jesus had a profound mistrust of all forcible methods of righting wrong, and that He consistently urged upon His followers a new and better way. If relationships should become strained by some

[1] Matt. vii. 12.
[2] Matt. xxii. 35–40.
[3] Matt. v. 9.
[4] Matt. v. 10–12. Note the word "falsely".
[5] Matt. v. 44.
[6] Matt. v. 9.
[7] Matt. v. 45.
[8] Matt. v. 48.

matter of personal dispute, then every possible effort must be made towards conciliation and agreement before appeal is made to the common law : "Agree with thine adversary quickly, whiles thou art with him in the way."[1] If an individual disciple should feel himself to be wronged by a "brother", that is by a fellow-believer, what is he to do ? His first duty is that of forgiveness unconditional and without limit : "Peter said to him, Lord, how oft shall my brother sin against me, and I forgive him ? until seven times ? Jesus saith unto him, I say not unto thee, Until seven times ; but, Until seventy times seven."[2] But, though for the wronged man forgiveness is a duty unconditional and unlimited, forgiveness can never be complete until it wins a response in the repentance of the wrongdoer, until the wrongdoer is won over and reconciliation is achieved. How is the wronged man to attain to this, in Jesus' eyes the only worthwhile, "redress" ? In another passage we have a hint : "If thy brother sin against thee, go, shew him his fault between thee and him alone : if he hear thee, thou hast gained thy brother. But if he hear thee not, take with thee one or two more, that at the mouth of two witnesses or three every word may be established. And if he refuse to hear thee, tell it unto the church : and if he refuse to hear the church also, let him be unto thee as the Gentile and the publican."[3] That is to say, the wronged man is not hastily to claim his right to the justice of the civil courts. Best of all, the initial act of forgiveness being assumed, he will by a personal approach remonstrate with his "brother", seek to clear away the misunderstanding, and thereby "win his brother" to his own viewpoint. Here we have the first hint of a truth to which we shall recur again and again : justice is truly vindicated, not when the wrongdoer is compelled to make reparation, but when the unjust will is "won" to justice.[4] If this best of all ways fails, the wronged man will seek a settlement by arbitration, preferably in private by one or two friends, if necessary through the mediation of the congregation of believers—but still without any recourse to the forcible sanctions of civil law. Only when all these efforts have failed is the wronged man to regard and treat the wrongdoer "as the Gentile and the publican".

Now what is the meaning of this last very puzzling injunction ? For it is difficult to believe that Jesus in using the words "Gentile" and "publican" in their commonly accepted opprobrious sense. I am again indebted to Principal Curtis for a very attractive suggestion: Only when all attempts at reconciliation have failed is the wronged Christian to "invoke the common law, which deals alike with

---

[1]Matt. v. 25.   [2]Matt. xviii. 21 f.   [3]Matt. xviii. 15–17.

[4]This "redemptive" element in the way of Jesus will be fully discussed in Chapter Six.

Gentiles, tax-gatherers, and believers. Let the law take its course in defeat of wrong only when religious instruments have failed. The Jew and the Christian should settle their differences without recourse to secular law ; they have a higher standard of right. When Jesus says, 'if he refuses to listen to the congregation let him be unto thee as a Gentile or a tax-gatherer', it is impossible to construe His mind in terms of an attitude to those men which He did not countenance or share, the ordinary Pharisaic attitude of excommunication or ostracism. He can only mean, 'descend to the common level of secular justice'. This corresponds to the repeated appeal which He makes that a Jew or a Christian will surely rise above the level of the standards in force among the people they have been taught to regard as below them, the Gentiles, sinners, and publicans."[1]

If this is permissible exegesis, then the passage may be not unfairly used to prove that Jesus did recognize the place of law in an ordered society, and under certain circumstances would approve appeal to its sanctions. But it is only as a last resort, when all the appeals of religion have been exhausted. The passage is chiefly significant as emphasizing that the distinctively Christian way of reacting to a wrong against oneself is very different from the instinctive demand of the natural man that "the law" should protect "his rights".

So much for the disciple's treatment of a "brother" who has wronged him. But everything which is most truly distinctive in the ethic of Jesus comes out most clearly when he lays down the principles which are to govern the Christian's reaction to a wrong against himself done not by a "brother", whom he may be expected to love, but by an "enemy", whom he may be supposed to suspect and dislike. Even here the second of the two "great commandments"[2] is to apply : even the "enemy" is a neighbour to be loved. As Joh. Weiss well says, "This is the highest demand that can ever be made . . . the love of enemy is not just one virtue among many, but the fairest flower of all human conduct,"[3] It is the "fruit" by which it shall be known whether or no Jesus' ethic is ruling a man's life.[4]

We thus arrive at what is admittedly the key-passage for our study, the "non-resistance" and "love-your-enemy" sections in Matthew v. 38–48 : "Ye have heard that it was said, An eye for an eye, and a tooth for a tooth : but I say unto you, Resist not him that is evil. . . . Ye have heard that it was said, Thou shalt love thy neighbour, and hate thine enemy : but I say unto you, Love your enemies, and pray for them that persecute you ; that you may be

[1]Matt. v. 46 f. ; vi. 32 ; Luke vi. 32 f., etc.   [3]*Commentary*, on Matt. v. 43 ff.
[2]Matt. xxii. 36 ff.   [4]Matt. vii. 20.

sons of your Father which is in heaven." Reserving meantime the question of the relevance of these sayings to wider social and national relationships, we shall probably be agreed that the primary reference is to the *personal* enemy, and that, however the words are to be interpreted, Jesus is here laying down, and consciously and deliberately doing so, a new principle, distinctively Christian and alternative to the commonly accepted one, which is to govern the meeting and overcoming of evil in our personal relationships. This can hardly be denied without evacuating what we have called the "antitheses of the Sermon on the Mount"[1] of all their meaning. Evil is now to be overcome, not by all those forcible methods which are commonly slumped together under the definition of "resistance", and by which it is thought that an exact retributive justice, a tit for tat, "an eye for an eye and a tooth for a tooth", will be exacted from the wrongdoer, but by the power of forbearing and, if necessary, suffering love. Paul perfectly paraphrases the Master when he writes : "Render to no man evil for evil. . . . Be not overcome of evil, but overcome evil with good."[2] How this new and better way caught the imagination of the primitive Church appears from the constant echoes of Jesus' words in the Apostolic writings.[3]

We note first that the two paragraphs, Matt. v. 38–42 ("resist not him that is evil"), and Matt. v. 43–8 ("love your enemies"), belong together as a single whole. The apparently negative injunction to non-resistance is immediately followed by the positive commandment of all-embracing love. No one who realizes this could caricature Jesus' words, as if He meant, "Acquiesce in evil. Be passively polite to wrongdoers. Tolerate vice. Allow the bully to rape his victim, and stand by with folded arms while he does so." The Pacifism of Jesus, if use the word we must, is never "passivism". And yet "resist not him that is evil", rightly understood, may be the indispensable pre-requisite to "love your enemies". There are times when a resolute refusal, merely negative though it seems, is the only possible foundation for an act of positive obedience, when a "yes" to the commandment of love must be preceded by a "no" to certain means and methods which must inevitably render that obedience abortive. It is only, says Jesus, when the old way has been renounced, that the new way can be explored.

If we are willing to take these things at their face value, then the way of Jesus would appear so clear that the wayfaring Christian,

[1]Above, p. 16.
[2]Rom. xii. 17–21. Some scholars think that the logic of Jesus' argument requires "retaliate not upon evil" rather than "resist not evil", and that the original Aramaic may have run : "You have heard that it was said, An eye in return for an eye, and a tooth in return for a tooth. But I say unto you, Do not render evil in return for evil." St. Paul's words would then be almost a literal echo of Jesus'.
[3]See *Appendix*, p. 109 f., "Christ's Way of Meeting Evil."

even though a fool, could hardly err therein. Yet this ethic—non-resistance, forbearance in the face of aggressive evil, love of enemies —is so sublime that we must all humbly confess with Heering that "only he who has believed in and experienced the redemptive love of God which Christ has revealed can truly understand and practise the Christian ethic ; the two together make up the Christian life, one indivisible whole. Thus it is that the lofty and powerful claims of the Gospel ring out as self-evident truths. They are self-evident to the man who is laid hold of by God in Christ, even though—since his salvation is never finished on earth, but is always only 'in hope'— he can only live up to them in small measure, and follow Christ only from afar."[1] Yet with reference to our present problem nothing is more important than that we should ask, "What *is* the teaching of Jesus ?" before we confuse the issue by going on to ask, "Is it practicable for us today to follow that teaching ?" It will therefore be useful to glance at some of the attempts which have been made to "water down" these "self-evident truths", and thereby to "keep on good terms with the Gospel",[2] while still countenancing methods which the Gospel has made obsolete. The fact that there is a certain measure of truth in some of these attempts will perhaps help us to correct and clarify our own interpretation.

(1) It is sometimes suggested that the "exaggerated" demands of Jesus are to be explained, if not explained away, on the ground of His "eschatological" outlook, that is His supposed belief in the immediate break-up of the present world-order. The injunctions of the Sermon on the Mount may be safely "short-circuited" once it is realized that they are inspired by the expectation of a speedy end to the world, that they contain only an ethic for the short time between Jesus' own day and that end, an "interim-ethic" as it is called, and that therefore they are not valid for those who do not share Jesus' historical perspective.

But, quite apart from the fact that this argument, if valid, would foreclose our whole enquiry by denying that we can ever propound an ethic for today based on Jesus' teaching,[3] modern scholars are inclined to agree that the supposed effect of "apocalyptic" upon

[1]Heering, op. cit. p. 26 f.

[2]The phrase is again Heering's, op. cit. p. 32.

[3]"To argue that Jesus' more general principles . . . were so dependent upon the limitations of His historical outlook that they lose their validity for practical conduct as soon as those limitations are transcended, and must not be allowed to interfere with the supposed necessities of modern economics and political life, is virtually to deny that there can be any such thing as a modern Christian ethic founded on the teaching of Jesus." C. J. Cadoux, *The Early Church and the World*, p. 13.

C

Jesus' moral teaching has been grossly exaggerated.[1] It may even be argued that the vivid expectation of the end of the age, so character- istic of the years immediately after Jesus, is the effect rather than the cause of these "exaggerated" demands of the New Testament ethic : a world which contemptuously rejected them was bound, Christians felt, to meet its doom.[2] Moreover, it is surely significant that Jesus urges this distinctive ethic, not in view of the immediate end of the age, but, as we have seen, on the ground that it is consistent with His own conception of God's nature,[3] surely a permanent element in His teaching if anything is. In any case the "interim-ethic" theory, even if valid, could at most suggest a doubt whether Jesus' teaching is valid under modern conditions. It does not touch our present question, What *is* that teaching ? Indeed, so far as the question of war is concerned, the "eschatological" argu- ment tells in a direction quite opposite to that intended by the critics of Pacifism ; for it does much to explain some of the perplex- ing "silences" of Jesus and the early Church concerning social and political problems.[4]

(2) It is argued, secondly, that these crucial sayings, like so much of Jesus' teaching, were spoken *ad hoc*, with reference to particular individuals in particular circumstances, and are not to be exalted into general principles binding upon all Christians. Now this is undoubtedly true of some of Jesus' most drastic demands. The command, for example, to "go, sell whatsoever thou hast, and give to the poor", is given specifically to the "Rich Young Ruler", for the special reason that in wealth Jesus saw for him the chief obstacle to discipleship.[5] But a saying with its special setting in a "Pro- nouncement Story"[6] is in a somewhat different category from those "timeless" sayings, without narrative framework, of which the Sermon on the Mount almost entirely consists, unless we go so far as to deny that Jesus ever laid down any general principles for universal application. It is noticeable that many of His most striking

[1]"The influence of eschatology on the ethics of the Gospel, especially on the Sermon on the Mount, is not so great as often even I myself have asserted it to be." (Windisch, *Der Sinn der Bergpredigt*, p. 152.) So also C. G. Montefiore : "It is an important fact, and one of which we must take adequate note, that there is a good deal of Jesus' religious and ethical teaching which was not directly related to, or dependent upon any eschatological conceptions, any belief in the nearing end of the world . . . a good deal in His finest religious and ethical teaching which can survive such conceptions and be easily detached from them." This Jewish scholar then adds : "What is remarkable about the sayings of the Gospels is that they are often applicable to wholly alien conditions, and true even without that belief in the end of the world which underlies so many of them . . . no surer mark of their genius and first-classness." (*Synoptic Gospels*, Vol. II, p. 114.)

[2]Cf. Col. iii. 6, etc.

[3]Matt. v. 45, 48.   [5]Mark x. 21.

[4]See below, p. 45, and above, p. 19.   [6]See p. 19.

and compelling sayings have been preserved in isolation without any narrative setting : they were felt to be so challenging, so universally binding, that no "story" was necessary to point the application.[1]

(3) But, it is asked again, should not these sayings be considered as merely highly-coloured illustrations of a general principle, in this case the principle that "intensity" or "screwing up the standard"[2] is a necessity in all Christian practice ? Now it must again be admitted that Jesus commonly made use of characteristic Semitic hyperbole ; and this argument may possibly be valid in the case of an isolated and obvious verbal hyperbole (e.g. Luke xiv. 26, "If any man . . . *hateth* not his own father"), or when a proposition stated literally (e.g. Matt. v. 28, "Every one that looketh on a woman to lust after her . . .") is then pointedly illustrated by an obvious metaphor (e.g. "If thy right eye causeth thee to stumble, pluck it out"). But such an explanation is surely most unlikely in the case of teaching deliberately chosen to illustrate the "fulfilment" of the "law" by Jesus,[3] and the showing forth of the Divine nature in human conduct,[4] particularly (and this cannot be too strongly stressed) when that teaching is so entirely and literally in line with Jesus' own way of life. It may, of course, be freely admitted that "turning the other cheek" is a hyperbolic Semitic illustration of a general principle : but that principle itself is stated, as one universally valid, in the opening words of each paragraph, "Resist not him that is evil" . . . "Love your enemies." Such considerations seem conclusive against all such attempts to suggest that Jesus' distinctive method of meeting evil, and the sayings which commend it, must be understood not literally but "spiritually", which really amounts to saying "*cum grano salis*". It is too often the case that "what is stoutly called the 'spirit' of the Sermon is rather its abrogation" ; and with reference to our present problem such methods are only too apt to result in "war-exegesis".[5]

(4) It is suggested, finally, that we have here "counsels of perfection" intended to apply, not to the present world, but to the Kingdom of God which is still to come. They are valid only in a perfect society. Meantime we are living, not in the Kingdom of God, but in a national state, which is a mediating conception, a compromise if we will, maintained by the authority of law, between the anarchy of brute force and that regime of pure grace which is the ultimate Christian ideal. Meanwhile we must be content to follow

---

[1]Cf. Matt. xi. 25–30 ; Mark viii. 34 ff. How the general saying about "taking the cross" is given a particular application in a "Pronouncement Story" is seen in Mark x. 21.

[2]The phrase is Montefiore's ; *Synoptic Gospels*, Vol. I, p. 25.

[3]Matt. v. 17.   [4]Matt. v. 45.

[5]Baumgarten, quoted by Windisch, *Theol. Rundschau*, 1951, pp. 333, 345.

the way of Jesus only to the extent that it is possible under the conditions of human existence which God Himself has created and still permits. Under these conditions the ethic of the Sermon, even if it literally represents the mind of Christ, is for the community as a whole so impracticable as to be utterly impossible of adoption as a practical way of life even by the Christian Church. In other words, the Church is justified in postponing obedience to the way of Jesus until the coming of the Kingdom makes such obedience so easy that it becomes "practicable" for the whole community.

Now, apart from the fact that much of the Sermon would be irrelevant in a perfect society, where presumably there would be no wrongs to submit to and no enemies to love,[1] this argument obscures one of the most characteristic features of all Jesus' teaching. Nowhere in the Gospels is it suggested that disciples are to postpone obedience until such obedience can be universalized. Rather are they definitely challenged to act in the spirit of Jesus in advance of the community. They are to go the "extra mile"[2] along a road which the world may call illogical, impracticable, quixotic. Otherwise "what do ye more than others ?"[3] Admittedly we do not live in that ideal world which would make easy the way of Christ. But, as someone has well said, "the Christian must learn to live not as a baffled idealist but as a rebel against the world as it is." The Gospel of the Kingdom is not only an ideal, but a method of attaining that ideal. For Jesus, too, the Kingdom was still in the future. But that did not prevent Him from preaching a "realized eschatology",[4] and bidding His disciples here and now order their lives by the laws of the coming Kingdom, promising them that if they did so the Kingdom would break in upon them and take them unawares.[5] As Heering caustically says, "There is no more effective way of disabling the Gospel than first to relegate the fulfilment of Christ's commands to the Kingdom of God, and then to read His saying, My Kingdom is not *of* this world, as if He had said, My Kingdom is not *for* this world."[6] That the primitive Church regarded Jesus' words as injunctions to be taken literally and

[1]"It is impossible to love a person except by loving him now ; a love which proposed to operate a few years hence, or 'hereafter in a better world than this', is plainly not love at all . . . Whence it follows that . . . this present world comes to have the most solemn significance as the scene where the obligations of the Kingdom of God in a personal order are laid upon us, and we must surrender ourselves utterly to God in their discharge." H. H. Farmer, *The World and God*, p. 216.

[2]Matt. v. 41.

[3]Matt. v. 47.

[4]See C. H. Dodd, *The Apostolic Preaching and its Developments*, 1936, pp. 208 ff.

[5]Matt. xii. 28 ; Luke xi. 20.

[6]Heering, op. cit. p. 34.

practised here and now is perfectly clear from passage after passage.[1]
Did not Jesus in His own Person set such an example ?[2]

We turn therefore from Jesus' teaching to His example ; for Jesus
was what He taught, so that the best commentary upon His words
is His life, just as the best interpretation of His life is His words.
How then do we find Jesus in His own Person meeting and overcoming evil ? Though He consistently lived by a principle of "non-
resistance", yet there was nothing negative about His life. He never
belittled or condoned the stark reality of evil : but He never met it
with its own methods and weapons. He overcame evil with good.
Nowhere, with the very doubtful exception of the Cleansing of the
Temple,[3] do we find Him using force to constrain men to desist
from evil or to do good ; nor, with the exception of one very
ambiguous passage,[4] countenancing the use of force even in self-
defence. On the contrary we see Him in His own Person proving
again and again that active love can win moral victories where
society, with its conventional methods of coercion and penalty, was
helpless. We think of the Gerasene "demoniac",[5] the woman who
was a sinner,[6] the woman taken in adultery,[7] Zacchaeus,[8] the dying
thief.[9] Of this aspect of Jesus' teaching the famous French scholar
Loisy writes, "A country where all the honest folk conformed to
these maxims would be a paradise of thieves and scoundrels." He
seems to have forgotten the actual effect on "thieves and scoundrels"
when Jesus Himself so dealt with them. It is pertinent to ask
whether Jesus *could* have so succeeded, if He had *also* backed
righteousness by violent methods, if He had been ready to stone
the adultress and only afterwards to forgive her, to crucify the
thief before He promised Him Paradise. Would the world have
hailed Him as Saviour if He had died leading the Jewish patriots
against the Roman legions instead of forgiving His enemies upon a
Roman Cross ? For this positive redemptive method of overcoming
evil, when carried to the uttermost, finds its supreme illustration in
the Cross, where Jesus refused the method of force in dealing with
the world's evil and prayed for His enemies instead, thereby setting
forth in action the power of suffering and sacrificial love to vindicate
the moral order and recreate a sinful world.[10]

It is sometimes asked whether the verdict on Jesus' pacifist
teaching and example must not be qualified in the light of certain

---

[1]Cf. Rom. xii. 14 ff. ; 1 Cor. iv. 12 ; vi. 7 ; 1 Thess. v. 15   1 Pet. iii. 8 f.
[2]1 Pet. ii. 21 ff.
[3]See p. 17 f. above.
[4]See p. 22 f. above.
[5]Mark v. 2 ff.
[6]Luke vii. 36 ff.
[7]John viii. 3 ff.
[8]Luke xix. 1 ff.
[9]Luke xxiii. 39 ff.
[10]The bearing of the Cross on our subject is fully discussed in Chapter Six.

violently denunciatory sayings against, for example, the Pharisees,[1] Herod,[2] the man who "causes little ones to stumble".[3] Does not such denunciation show that Jesus was, to say the least, an inconsistent Pacifist ? Does it not imply an attitude of anger and hatred which in appropriate circumstances might result in even acts of violence ? We may take the denunciation of the Pharisees as a test case, and perhaps the following considerations will suffice :

(a) It is almost certain that these denunciatory sayings have been heightened by Jesus' reporters, particularly by Matthew, who is throughout his Gospel strongly anti-Pharisaic. A comparison of Matthew xxiii. with the parallel passages in Mark and Luke[4] shows that the Markhan and Lukan versions are much briefer and much less "offensive". It seems clear that Matthew has sought to heighten the effect of the denunciation by adding other sayings of doubtful relevance. For example, the words in Matthew xxiii. 33, "ye serpents, ye offsprings of vipers", occur, according to Luke,[5] in an address of John the Baptist, and Matthew appears to have transferred them to Jesus.[6] Matthew, moreover, certainly records the denunciation in a vindictive spirit : "He detested the Pharisees, and gloried in the hard things Jesus had said about them."[7]

(b) There is obviously an ethical distinction between the sternest rebuke and recourse to physical violence. Yet it may be fairly objected that consistent Pacifism implies the renunciation not only of violence but of the spirit of hatred which so often prompts it. Nevertheless, righteous anger is not inconsistent with a Pacifist ethic, when it is prompted not by malice but by a love which embraces within its redemptive purpose even the object of denunciation. It is clear that Jesus' anger here had two causes : the conviction firstly, that Pharisaic hypocrisy (i.e. the contrast between profession and practice) was one of the most serious obstacles to the effectiveness of His own message, and, secondly, that it was leading the Pharisees themselves to destruction. The expression, "Woe unto you !" so far from being a "curse" is expressive, not so much of anger as of pity, and might well be translated, "Alas for you !" The aim of Jesus' denunciation was to turn His victims back from

[1]Matt. xxiii., especially verse 33, "Ye serpents, ye offsprings of vipers, how shall ye escape the judgement of Hell ?"
[2]Luke xiii. 32, "that fox".
[3]Matt. xviii. 6, "It is profitable for him that a millstone should be hanged about his neck, and that he should be sunk in the depth of the sea."
[4]Mark xii. 38–40 ; Luke xx. 45–7 ; xi. 37–52.
[5]Luke iii. 7.
[6]The metaphor is vividly apposite in Luke, where the crowds fleeing from "the wrath" are likened to snakes wriggling away from a fire in the heather. It is quite out of place when applied by Matthew to the Pharisees.
[7]See an article by W. E. Wilson in *Reconciliation*, July, 1934, p. 183.

unreality to truth, and so to save not only their dupes but themselves.

(c) The denunciatory sayings must in their turn be qualified by Jesus' express rebuke of all censorious judgment.[1] True, the presence of these two strands in Jesus' teaching has sometimes been made the ground for charging Him with "inconsistency".[2] But the fact that our own anger is in ninety-nine cases out of a hundred tinged with censoriousness must not blind us to the possibility that He, who was Himself the "Truth" and the "Life", might be moved by an anger prompted by pure love of truth and a selfless passion to save those in peril of spiritual death.

What, then, is our conclusion concerning the way of Jesus in personal relationships ? Though by no definite pronouncement does He either abrogate the function of Law in an ordered society, or explicitly refuse to countenance under any conditions a moral use of force, yet it is clear from both His teaching and His example that His distinctive method of meeting and overcoming evil rests upon presuppositions which are very different. Evil can be truly conquered only by the power of truth and goodness and self-sacrificing love. The moral order can be vindicated, not by forcible restraint and punishment of the evil-doer, but only when the will which has defied that order is redeemed from its evil purpose. In the light of Jesus' ethic of absolute love, of His theology of a Father God to whom every individual human soul is infinitely precious, and finally of this redemptive method of overcoming evil, it is obvious that His way will permit the use of force only within the strictest limits. Under such principles the very essence of ethical living is reverence for human personality and loving discrimination towards one's fellow-men. If under the ethic of Jesus force ever finds a proper place in personal relations, it can only be in a form which leaves ample room for this sensitive discrimination and this redemptive purpose of an all-embracing love. We are thus prepared to consider the wider application of this New Testament ethic, and its bearing upon the specific problems of war.

[1]Matt. vii. 1 ff.
[2]See, e.g. the charge made by the Jewish scholar C. G. Montefiore ; *Synoptic Gospels*, Vol. II, p. 301.

CHAPTER FOUR

THE WIDER APPLICATION OF THE NEW TESTAMENT ETHIC: JESUS AND WAR

IS there any evidence that this distinctive method of meeting evil, which is so clearly laid down for His disciples in their personal relationships, was intended by Jesus to cover also a wider field of social and even national relationships ? This is quite commonly denied even by Christian expositors, and the argument usually takes one of two lines.

Sometimes it is argued that Jesus propounded this ethic as a rule of life to be practised within the community of His own disciples, but that He never contemplated that it should be unconditionally practised even by Christians in their contacts with the outside world. Or, to put it otherwise, the disciple *as a disciple* is bound by the "new way", but in the ordinary daily affairs of secular life, when he is acting not in the capacity of a disciple, but in the capacity of an ordinary "man in the street", there must be many occasions when he cannot be expected to practise this way. Or again, certain forcible methods are held to have been definitely renounced by Jesus so far as they might have been used *for the advancement of His Kingdom*, which is "not of this world" : but such methods might still be legitimate in His eyes, and even necessary, if practised by the rulers of a worldly kingdom. To illustrate : when Jesus said, "Whosoever would become great among you shall be your servant,"[1] the standard set up is valid only *within the Christian brotherhood*, and has no relevance beyond it. Or when He repels the Devil on the Mount of Temptation,[2] He is rejecting methods which He feels to be unworthy *for the furtherance of a spiritual Kingdom* or *for the sacred end He had in view*, but He is passing no judgment on such methods when used by earthly potentates. Or when He says, "The rulers of the Gentiles lord it over them, and their great ones exercise authority over them. Not so shall it be among you,"[3] He is not in any way critizing the kind of "authority" exemplified among the Gentiles, but is only insisting that *among His followers, in the Church*, brothers are not to exercise this kind of "authority," or "lord it" over their brethren. From this it is only a short step to argue that the words, "Put up again thy sword into its place : for all they that

[1]Matt. xx. 26.　　　　[2]Matt. iv. 8 ff.　　　　[3]Matt. xx. 25 f.

take the sword shall perish with the sword,"[1] imply that it is fatal
to use violent methods *to advance religious ends*, but have no relevance to the use of arms in ordinary life, much less to warfare
between nation and nation. In a word Jesus' distinctive ethic is
framed with a view to ruling man's *religious life*, not his everyday
contacts with his fellows.

Now it cannot be too strongly insisted that this "sacred-secular"
distinction would have been quite meaningless to Jesus ; indeed it
would have been so to any good Jew of Jesus' day. For if there was
one thing characteristic of contemporary Judaism it was that
religion was felt to be co-extensive with life. For the Jew his peculiar
doctrine of revelation implied "the bringing of all life under the
control of the revealed will of God. God had a word . . . for each
aspect of life however trivial. There would logically be no distinction
between the sacred and the secular. . . . It is an anomaly to speak of
the social or the ethical implications of this religion, because Judaism
held that social and ethical as well as 'religious' relations were
explicit rather than implicit in revelation. In its main developments
Judaism represents, accordingly, perhaps the most thoroughgoing
attempt in all history to order the whole of life by religion."[2] Are we
to think that Jesus confined "religion" within narrower limits than
did the pious Jew of His own day ? It is inconceivable that Jesus, as
a Jew, should formulate an ethic for a "spiritual" kingdom within
men's hearts, without contemplating that its imperative should be
co-extensive with life itself.

But a much more common line of argument is that the Gospel of
Jesus, or at any rate this particular ethic of "non-resistance" and
"love of enemies", is absolutely individualist and has no reference to
the wider relationships of the social community, least of all to the
dealings of nation with nation. To many, perhaps most, interpreters
of the Gospels it is almost a commonplace that Jesus had no concern
whatever with the social problems and national politics of His day.
His absorbing interest lay in the moral and spiritual life of individual
men and women. So far as He sought to redeem society He did so
exclusively by the indirect method of redeeming individual men.
The idea of the "Kingdom" in Jesus' thought had no social or
national reference whatever, but had to do with individual, inward,
and spiritual realities only. Thus the State and all those problems
which are our present study are held to be entirely outside the orbit
of His thought, and similarly outside the scope of His ethic. This is
the conclusion, for example, of Troeltsch : "From this point of view

[1]Matt. xxvi. 52.
[2]Macgregor and Purdy, *Jew and Greek : Tutors unto Christ*, p. 73. Cf. Moore,
Judaism, Vol. I, p. 112, etc.

we can see plainly the attitude of Jesus towards the State. . . . There is no thought of the State at all. Jewish nationalism and all its expectations are ignored entirely, even though Israel appears as the germ of the new world that is to be."¹ I am convinced that this is a disastrously mistaken conclusion, and that we shall never rightly evaluate the wider bearing of Jesus' ethic until we set it once again in its true historical perspective. If we are to do this, due weight must be given to the following considerations :

(1) By Jesus' contemporaries the "Kingdom of God" was undoubtedly contemplated as being the rule of God exercised over a concrete community, and was bound up with certain quite definitely national aspirations. We have no reason to suppose that John the Baptist departed in this respect from the current conception of the Kingdom, even though he warned his hearers not to presume upon their status as a chosen people.² Indeed the reason why John's appeal evoked such immediate response was probably because it brought to a focus the generally recognized type of expectation, though certainly with an increased moral emphasis. Jesus undoubtedly during the course of His ministry introduced into His teaching about the Kingdom new elements which enlarged and ennobled the whole conception.³ But the Gospels make it quite clear that at the beginning of His mission He carried forward virtually unchanged the main stresses of John's message.⁴ And though Jesus, too, insisted that Jewish nationality alone was no guarantee of the possession of the Kingdom, He still declared that it should be "given to a *nation* bringing forth the fruits thereof".⁵ Thus Jesus seems to have accepted and worked upon the universal assumption that the Kingdom would find its outward expression in a theocratic national community. Indeed, had He not done so, He must have been largely unintelligible. Had He taken over the idea of the Kingdom and read into it a completely other meaning, without having given clear indication that He was so doing, He could have only misled His hearers. Instead we find no evidence, at any rate in the earliest records, that He sought to disabuse His followers of the "delusion" that the Kingdom was to find its seat in a concrete community. However "spiritual" His conception of the Kingdom might be, His followers were still to pray : "May thy Kingdom come, may thy will be done, as in heaven, *so on earth*."⁶ Clearly then it is perilous to

¹*Social Teaching*, etc. ; quoted by C. J. Cadoux in an article on "The Politics of Jesus" in *The Congregational Quarterly*, January, 1936, p. 58. This is an admirable study to which I am much indebted.
²Matt. iii. 9.
³For this see C. H. Dodd, *The Parables of the Kingdom*, especially Chapter 2.
⁴Compare Matt. iii. 1 f. with Matt. iv. 17.
⁵Matt. xxi. 43.   ⁶Matt. vi. 10.

underline the purely spiritual and inward element in Jesus' teaching to the complete elimination of the social and political elements, or to argue, as for example does Dr. James Mackinnon, that "Jesus was too spiritually minded to concern Himself with the crass politics of the time. His absorbing interest lay in the moral and spiritual life."[1] Certainly it did : but it was in the spiritual life of the citizens of a community renewed and transformed because obedient to the new ethic of the Kingdom.

(2) In line with this is the undoubted fact that Jesus addressed His teaching in the first instance to His own Jewish compatriots. He definitely confined His ministry and that of His immediate circle to Palestine.[2] His Twelve Companions are to "sit upon twelve thrones, judging the twelve tribes of Israel".[3] Almost regretfully, but still firmly, He insists that He "was not sent but unto the lost sheep of the house of Israel".[4] We note, too, that Jesus had the habit of contrasting His followers, not with irreligious men in general, but simply with "the Gentiles" : "If ye salute your brethren only, what do ye more than others ? Do not even the Gentiles the same ?"[5] "In praying do not go babbling on, as the Gentiles do,"[6] "Be not therefore anxious saying, What shall we eat . . . ? For after all these things do the Gentiles seek."[7] "They which are accounted to rule over the Gentiles lord it over them. . . . But it is not so among you."[8] As Dr. Cadoux well says, "The only natural antithesis to the Gentiles as such is Israel as such : and I can therefore make no sense of these passages except on the assumption that Jesus addressed His appeal to the Jews *qua* Jews, in distinction (for the time being) from the Gentile world."[9] No doubt the whole spirit of Jesus' teaching was such that Paul and the Church were certainly reflecting His mind, when they stressed the universal significance of the Gospel, and its removal of all barriers between Jew and Gentile. Yet it is clear that Jesus had a plan for His own people which was integrally bound up with His idea of the Kingdom, that He must have been profoundly concerned in the social and national problems which were crucial for His people at the time, and that His ethical teaching must have been framed with those problems in view, and with a definite bearing upon them.

[1] *The Historic Jesus*, p. 49.
[2] Matt. x. 5 f.
[3] Matt. xix. 28.
[4] Matt. xv. 24.
[5] Matt. v. 47 ; the word "sinners" in Luke vi. 32 ff. is clearly less original, and is in line with Luke's pro-Gentile bias.
[6] Matt. vi. 7.
[7] Matt. vi. 32.
[8] Mark x. 42 f.
[9] *The Congregational Quarterly*, January, 1936, p. 60.

(3) If one fact about Jesus is agreed upon by moderate scholars, it is that He thought of Himself as Messiah. Those who doubt this do so only because Messiahship for Him clearly meant so much more than it did to the average Jew, that the title might seem more likely to be bestowed upon Him by His disciples than appropriated by Himself. But this is virtually to reject the entire historical framework of the Gospels, and thereby foreclose our whole discussion. Now, to whatever extent Jesus may have modified, and did modify, the conception of Messiahship, of one feature He could not deprive it, without evacuating it of its whole significance and making its claim meaningless to His hearers : and that feature was the national character of the rôle. No man in Jesus' day could claim the title of Messiah without at once being brought face to face, by the pressure of public opinion and the eager enquiries of tentative followers, with a national and political problem of the first magnitude. And this must have been so even in the case of Jesus, however true it may be that "His absorbing interest lay in the moral and spiritual life". This problem was the attitude to be taken up by the pious Jew to the alien and hated rulers of his country. And while the whole nation, with the possible exception of the Sadducees and the Herodians, was keenly exercised by this problem—Zealots, Pharisees, the "quiet of the land" alike—it is really incredible that Jesus, as claimant to the Messiahship, could have ignored the problem so entirely as many scholars believe, or could have failed to suggest a solution of it, and indicate the bearing upon it of His general ethical principles. "It is no exaggeration to say that the mind of Israel was in Jesus' day *obsessed* with the political issue : and the only inference we can draw from the fact that Jesus had a plan for the Jews to fulfil on earth, is that *He had something to say to them about the political issue* that obsessed them. His acknowledgment to Pilate that He held a royal office surely puts this beyond question."[1]

(4) It is just at this point that we find justification for extending the scope of Jesus' distinctive ethic to cover the actual question of war, and indeed for believing that Jesus Himself must have consciously so applied it. "The most important characteristic of His Messiahship, speaking negatively, is to be found in His refusal to wage the Messianic war."[2] And this, although leadership in such a war was precisely what His followers would expect of Messiah. Such an overthrow of the Gentile empire by the might of God's Anointed had been foretold both by the Old Testament prophets and by the Jewish Apocalyptic writings ; and however opinions differed as between Zealots, Pharisees and the "quiet of the land" as to the best way to hasten such a victory, it was universally associated with the

---

[1]Cadoux, in loc. cit. p. 61.   [2]Windisch, *Der Mess. Krieg*, p. 95.

appearance of Messiah. And in Jesus' day, to quote Cadoux once more, this expectation "was still further supported by the normal human view of tyrant empires and unwilling subjects : no one could deny that there was a good *casus belli*. Whatever, therefore, was the solution Jesus offered, it must have been fashioned in some direct relation, either positive or negative, to the prevailing expectation regarding the conquering Messiah's rôle." Yet Jesus utterly refused to contemplate such a war : His solution was that Israel should"turn away from desiring vengeance against Rome and destruction for the Gentiles, should meekly submit for the time being to servitude and injustice, and, trusting wholly to deeds of love and words of truth, should undercut pagan hostility, outmanœuvre political lordship, convert enemies to friends, and stand forth in the name and power of God as the heralds and propagators of the one true religioun."[1]

Why, we may ask, did Jesus thus renounce the expected Messianic war ? Not merely, we may be sure, because He was convinced that such an appeal was doomed to failure. He was obviously willing to die for His cause. Why not in arms, if He knew His cause to be just and believed that the war-method might be right ? Not even, as has often been argued, because such action might seem to be a presumptuous anticipation of the expected supernatural breaking-in of the Power of God, who was Himself to "give the Kingdom".[2] The good Jew never fought the less valiantly himself because he believed that Yahweh alone could give the victory.[3] No ! so far as we can see, the refusal of Jesus to wage war as Messiah was due first and foremost to the fact that, in spite of all the precedents provided by the Old Testament, He regarded the war-method as inherently evil, a violation of His own supreme commandment to love one's neighbour as oneself, and a *reductio ad absurdum* of His basic principle that the motive of all Christian discipleship is to be "a son of your Father which is in heaven",[4] and so to reflect in some poor measure the nature of the God who "maketh His sun to rise on the evil and the good" alike.

[1]Cadoux, in loc. cit. pp. 61, 62.

[2]Luke xii. 32.

[3]It may, however, be noted that the apocalyptic expectations both of Jesus and of the early Church have a real bearing on the comparative silence of the Gospels concerning the applicability of Jesus' ethic to social and political questions, a silence which our opponents have not been slow to turn to account. "The eschatological outlook . . . resulted in Christianity not demanding the realization of its principles in society and State for fear of destruction or failure. Had the first missionaries been told that the world was to go on existing for long, long ages yet, and that Christ would not return though centuries pass, they would not have been able, with good conscience, to let the world go on taking the course it did take." (Harnack, *Militia Christi*, p. 50).

[4]Matt. v. 45.

(5) Thus to place the great sayings of Jesus against this wider background of the life of His nation is not to rob them of their higher spiritual qualities : it is only to insist that one cannot rightly interpret them till they are first set in their true historical perspective ; and it is to discover additional point and colour in passage after passage. Even when the main bearing of a saying is upon the ordering of life within the Fellowship, there is an inevitable sideglance at the current national situation, and this very fact suggests that the sayings themselves are of wider application than is often admitted. For example :

(a) Though the chief importance of Jesus' Temptation is that it shows Him to us reaching the full realization of His "Sonship", and the conviction that for Him Messiahship must mean something very different from the popularly expected rôle, yet it is surely significant that Jesus defines to Himself the meaning of His mission by reference to the kind of dominion which He felt compelled to renounce : "The devil showeth him all the kingdoms of the world, and the glory of them ; and he said unto him, All these things will I give thee, if thou wilt fall down and worship me."[1] If there be any force in the argument of this chapter, then Jesus *did* feel Himself called by God to exercise authority over the life of the nations *as such*, and not only to wield a purely spiritual rule in men's hearts ; for wideworld rule over the nations was the Messiah's recognized destiny.[2] To refuse to "worship Satan" must then mean, not to renounce a national kingdom *simpliciter*, but to renounce "satanic" methods of winning that kingdom. What Jesus turned from, as morally wrong and disloyal to His vocation, was the one and only recognized way to empire in His own day, the way of the sword.

(b) Similarly, when Jesus sets up a new standard of greatness among His disciples with the words, "The rulers of the Gentiles lord it over them. . . . Not so shall it be among you,"[3] it is impossible to admit that He is not at the same time passing judgment on the kind of dominion exemplified by the pagan empire, a dominion won by warfare, exercised over unwilling subjects, and maintained by the power of armed force.

(c) The same background appears to lie behind the crucial sayings of the Sermon on the Mount. It has become a commonplace to assert that all the sayings in the section beginning, "Resist not him that is evil,"[4] are meant to govern the disciple in his private capacity, and leave untouched his duty as a member of society and of the nation. But this is hardly consistent with the fact that all three illustrations relate to *social* sanctions—the Lex Talionis which Jesus

[1]Matt. iv. 8 f.   [2]Isa. lx. 3, etc.   [3]Mark x. 42-5.   [4]Matt. v. 38 ff.

claims to transcend ;[1] the right to justice in the public courts ;[2] the liability to compulsory state labour. The last reference in particular —"whosoever shall compel thee to go one mile"[3]—vividly suggests the domineering bearing of the Roman or Herodian official. Indeed the background of the whole "non-resistance" section stares one in the face. Jesus' fellow-countrymen are to pursue the policy of reconciliation and peace with the foreign ruler, even at the risk of temporary submission to injustice.

(d) The same is true of the next paragraph containing the "love-your-enemy" sayings.[4] Once again it is commonly argued that the word "enemy" must be limited to the private enemy, or at any rate to the fellow-Jew-enemy.[5] The word used, it is pointed out, is not *polemios*, the foe in time of war, but *echthros*, one who stands in a relationship of personal hatred. This linguistic argument has little force, for *polemios* is nowhere used in the New Testament, whereas *echthros* is used both in the Septuagint and in the New Testament for the public as well as the personal enemy.[6] When we remember how Jesus extends the scope of the parallel word "neighbour",[7] it seems likely that He similarly enlarges the idea of an "enemy". If it be argued that the word "neighbour" in Leviticus xix. 18 (of which Matthew v. 43 is apparently an echo) is a technical term for a compatriot or fellow-Israelite, then it follows *a fortiori* that the command to love not only "neighbours" but "enemies" is a command not only to love compatriots even when enemies, but to love even the foreign enemy himself. The same inference may be drawn from the implied antithesis in verse 47, for "brethren" regularly means "fellow-Israelites", and suggests as its converse the "stranger" or "foreigner". Moreover all these sayings must be interpreted with reference to the environment in which they were presumably spoken ; that is in Galilee, the hot-bed of revolutionary nationalism, where armed resistance to the hated dominion of the foreigner was the burning question of the hour. Are we to believe that Jesus, claiming Himself to be Messiah, had nothing to say concerning the bearing of these crucial sayings upon this inter-racial enmity ? Thus Professor Windisch again, though himself no Pacifist, can write : "When Jesus bade His followers love their enemies, do good to them, pray for them, endure their attacks and provocations with meekness . . . He stifled every thought of rebellion and national

---

[1]Matt. v. 38–9.

[2]Matt. v. 40, which Paul accepted as something more than a hyperbolical Semitic metaphor, as seems clear from 1 Cor. vi. 7.

[3]Matt. v. 41 ; literally "impress" ; cf. Mark xv. 21 of Simon bearing the Cross.

[4]Matt. v. 43–8.

[5]See, e.g. Montefiore, *Synoptic Gospels*, Vol. II, p. 85.

[6]See Windisch, *Theol. Rundschau*, 1915, p. 345.

[7]Luke x. 29, ff.

war"[1] ; and, even in the heat of war-time, he feels compelled to admit that "it must not be overlooked that Pacifism, in applying the principles of the Gospel to the national enemy, seems better to agree with the spirit of Jesus".[2]

(e) Finally, many of the premonitions of national disaster, which the Gospels so often put upon Jesus' lips, take a new and a much more vivid colour, once we realize that Jesus is contemplating, not only the penalty of rejecting His spiritual Gospel, but also the dire consequences which are bound to fall upon His people, if they prefer militant nationalism to His own pacifist policy of patience, peace, and reconciliation. We may instance the lamentation over Jerusalem[3] ; the woes pronounced over the unrepentant Galilean towns[4] ; the warning concerning the reading of the signs of the weather[5] ; the advice to seize the first chance of reconciliation with one's adversary[6] ; the urgent call to repentance, driven home by the reference to Pilate's brutal massacre[7] ; the parable of the unfruitful fig-tree,[8] and of the wicked husbandmen[9] ; the prediction of the destruction of Jerusalem[10] ; and finally Jesus' ominous reply to the women who wept after Him on His way to the Cross, ending with the words, "If they do these things in the green tree, what shall be done in the dry ?"[11] Jesus unquestionably foresaw untold disaster for His people as a result of their rejection as a nation of His own pacifist ethic : and, doing so, can He possibly have omitted to apply that ethic explicitly to the national situation in His own day ?

(6) The place of the Cross in Jesus' redemptive purpose, and in the Christian doctrine of reconciliation and the conquest of evil, must be more fully discussed in Chapter Six. But the Cross has first to be considered as an event in history. And, historically speaking, the Cross was the direct consequence of Jesus' pacifist ethic alike in teaching and in practice : in teaching, because His Pacifism towards the Gentiles in General and Rome in particular would undoubtedly arouse the patriotic animus of the multitude, and so explain the sudden waning of His popularity and His ultimate betrayal to the authorities ; in practice, because the same principles which forbade rebellion against Rome also forbade violent resistance to His enemies on Jesus' own part. It was this that brought Jesus to the

[1]*Der Mess. Krieg*, p. 31.
[2] *Theol. Rundschau*, 1915, p. 346.
[3]Luke xix. 41-4.
[4]Matt. xi. 20 ff. ; Luke x. 13 ff.
[5]Luke xii. 54 ff.
[6]Luke xii. 58.
[7]Luke xiii. 1 ff.
[8]Luke xiii. 6 ff.
[9]Mark xii. 1 ff.
[10]Mark xiii. 1 ff. and the parallels.

[11]Luke xxiii. 27 ff. ; "I understand the obscure closing sentence to mean : If the Romans practise such cruelties as this crucifixion of me when peace is flourishing, what atrocities will they commit when it has withered away amid the storms of war ?" (Cadoux, in loc. cit. p. 64.)

Cross, while His own people yelled, "Not this man, but Barabbas," preferring the champion of armed revolution to the Lord of love.[1] The plain fact is that, because Jesus was *not* a Barabbas, He went to the Cross. It is probable indeed (to judge by such passages as Mark viii. 31, Mark ix. 31, etc.) that for some time before the crisis Jesus had already seen what His fate was bound to be, so that the Cross may well have presented itself to Him as the direct alternative to the waging of the Messianic war. By dying, and not by the warlike methods of popular expectation, would He proclaim to His nation His conception of Messiahship.[2]

This, no doubt, is a line of argument from which some will vigorously dissent. Christ died on the Cross, we are told, not as a result of His pacifist ethic, but simply as the world's predestined Redeemer ; He died "in obedience to the requirements of God". This may be perfectly true ; but we may not for that reason, by way of a facile theological truism, take a short cut past the factors which determined the Cross as an event in history. Jesus knew it to be His vocation to lead men to God, and to demonstrate His power to overcome evil, by the preaching and practice of an ethic of absolute love. He had set this before Himself as a definite alternative to the waging of the universally expected Messianic war. And by His death, not on the battlefield but on a Roman Cross. He sealed and consummated that alternative.

If our reasoning has been valid, then we must recognize that the principles which we have been studying, integral and fundamental as they are to Jesus' ethics, were consciously intended by Himself to have an application far wider than has often been admitted. Politics, the State, international relations all come within the orbit. In particular it may be suggested that an Historical Religion, at the centre of whose doctrine of reconciliation stands the Cross, can have no excuse for excluding from its ethics, national no less than individual, that distinctive method of confronting evil which brought about the occurrence of the Cross as an event in history. The Pacifism which led Jesus to the Cross is so integral a part of His

[1] The Greek word for "robber", which is used of Barabbas in John xviii. 40, is the word used most frequently by Josephus to describe the armed Zealot "revolutionaries".

[2] "He would have ruined His mission if He had encouraged the war-fever. The quickening of conscience which He invoked would have been lost. But He took upon Himself the consequences of the decision which, in opposition to the national ideal, He had arrived at. He endured, He suffered, He went to His death. And in spite of the Jews He became the Messiah triumphant. Without strife of arms, though He, too, was a fighter, the Galilean had conquered." (Windisch, *Der Mess, Krieg*, p. 80.)

D

whole attitude towards the life of individuals and of the nation alike, that it must also be recognized to be an integral part of any ethic which can in the full sense of the word claim to be Christian.[1]

[1]Dr. Cadoux concludes the article to which reference has been made thus : "The politics of Jesus were no mere incident or accident of His ministry ; they were interwoven with the most central things in His Gospel. It was His politics, more than anything else, that brought about His death ; and it was by and through the temporary defeat of death that His ultimate and eternal victory was won. That is why Christians believe His death to be the most central and important fact in history. But if they are right in so emphasizing the significance of His death, then surely the ethical principles, from which both the politics and the death resulted, ought to be emphasized as of central importance also."

See also Dr. Cadoux's book *The Historic Mission of Jesus*, Chapter VI.

CHAPTER FIVE

THE "WRATH" OF GOD

AT this point we pass from questions mainly of interpretation to those which are more strictly theological. And here we meet the challenge, which it has become fashionable for highly-placed ecclesiastics to fling at us, that Pacifism is a modern "heresy". On the face of it the charge is surprising, for "heresy" strictly speaking means false doctrine which has been formally condemned by the Church, whereas the facts are that the earliest Church was almost universally pacifist, and Christians have always assumed that it is not the pacifist, but rather the militarist, position which, from the Christian standpoint, required to be defended as "under certain circumstances" justifiable. Yet the late Archbishop William Temple has argued[1] that Pacifism is a recrudescence of three ancient Church heresies : "Manichaeism", because the Pacifist "makes a sharp contrast between spiritual and material forces, and holds that the material cannot be completely subordinated to the spiritual" ; "Marcionism", because he holds a "view of the New Testament as so superseding the Old Testament as to abolish it" ; and "Pelagianism", because he believes in "man's capacity apart from conversion and sanctification to obey the Counsels of Perfection . . . a view which regards man as capable by the action of his own will of living by love only." The first of these three "heresies" need not detain us, for if it is relevant at all it is so only to pure Tolstoyism (i.e. the complete renunciation of every kind of force), a creed which we believe to be an over-simplification of our own particular problem[2] ; and in any case it is surely not "heresy" to "deny that the use of matter for the indiscriminate murder of human beings is or can ever be a manifestation of the Spirit"[3]. The other two charges, however, bring us to the heart of our problem and must be frankly faced ; but perhaps we may first reformulate this charge of "heresy" in plain English under three counts :

Firstly, Pacifism misrepresents the character of God, and the revelation of Him in Jesus Christ, by slurring over the sterner side of the Divine nature ;

[1] *York Diocesan Leaflet*, 1935.
[2] For this see C. E. Raven, *Is War Obsolete ?* pp. 150 ff.
[3] C. E. Raven, in *Reconciliation*, December, 1935, p. 321.

Secondly, the Pacifist ethic unwarrantably exalts love at the expense of righteousness and justice ;

Thirdly, Pacifism misinterprets the true significance of the Cross. We shall deal with the first of these three charges in the present chapter and with the other two in Chapter Six.

Firstly, then, it is argued that Pacifism gives a one-sided picture of the Divine nature. Are there not, we are asked, certain aspects of God's character which may not be wholly revealed in the Person of Jesus Christ, and certain factors in God's way of dealing with evil which are not wholly evident in Jesus' way of meeting it as evidenced in the New Testament ? And may we not therefore be justified, in certain circumstances, in departing from the love-ethic, for which a warrant has been found in the New Testament—such departure even on occasion taking the form of participation in war ? In a word, are we not entitled to stress God's "wrath" as well as His love, to offer ourselves as the instruments of His punitive as well as of His reconciling activity ? It is clear that there are really two questions here : (1) What is the truth about this "sterner" side of the Divine nature ? What does the New Testament mean when it speaks of the "wrath" of God ? (2) In any case is it competent for the Christian to seek to imitate God on this side of His activity ?

(1) First, then, what has the New Testament to tell us about the sterner side of God's nature ? It is perfectly true that there are sayings of Jesus which suggest His belief in a God of stern justice as well as of infinite love. Does He not teach that there is a place for terrible severity as well as for long-suffering forbearance in the Divine providence? "Depart from me, ye cursed, into the eternal fire which is prepared for the devil and his angels"[1] ; "I tell you, I know not whence ye are ; depart from me, all ye workers of iniquity. There shall be weeping and gnashing of teeth"[2] ; "Whoso shall cause one of these little ones that believe on me to stumble, it is profitable for him that a great millstone should be hanged about his neck, and that he should be sunk in the depth of the sea"[3] ; "Rather fear Him which is able to destroy both soul and body in hell."[4] We think, too, of expressions like "our God is a consuming fire".[5] And through Paul's letters, especially that to the Romans, there run like a recurrent refrain references to the Divine "wrath" : "The wrath of God is revealed from heaven against all ungodliness and unrighteousness of men"[6] ; "Thou treasurest up for thyself wrath in the day of wrath and revelation of the righteous judgement of God ; who will render to every man according to his works"[7] ;

[1]Matt. xxv. 41.   [4]Matt. x. 28.
[2]Luke xiii. 27 f.   [5]Heb. xii. 29, taken over, of course, from Deut. iv. 24.
[3]Matt. xviii. 6.   [6]Rom. i. 18.   [7]Rom. ii. 5 f.

"For which things' sake cometh the wrath of God upon the sons of disobedience"[1] ; "The wrath is come upon them to the uttermost."[2] As we shall see, the crux of the problem is the correct understanding of the meaning of this word "wrath".

Over and above the Scriptural evidence we are quite fairly bidden by our critics to take account of the witness both of nature and of history to the stern retributory justice of God. Both these aspects of the problem must be more fully dealt with below. But first it will be well to lay down certain general principles ; and to begin with, as to our method of approach. Instead of asking, "How are these sterner elements in the Divine nature and Divine activity to be explained consistently with the revelation given in Jesus Christ ?" we shall do better to ask, "What are we to conceive to be the nature of God's purpose in creation, and of His problem in dealing with evil in general and human sin in particular ?"

Now from any theistic, not to say Christian, standpoint, must we not define this purpose and this problem as the creation of a moral universe of free persons, and the bringing of these persons into a right relationship both to their fellow-men and to God Himself ? Moreover, if men are to be so trained and disciplined, and yet at the same time are to remain free, it would appear that both in the environment or "field of operations" in which this education and development are to take place, and also in the working out of these mutual relationships, there must be elements and factors "independent", so to speak, of the immediate and moment-by-moment control of the will of God. That is to say, there may be, for example, catastrophes in the world of nature, and events in the field of history, which, while they happen within God's world and therefore must be said to be "permitted" by Him, yet cannot be ascribed to Him as the direct result of His immediate volitional purpose and activity. The necessity of this for the safeguarding of human freedom and human personality would appear to be less obvious in the world of nature than in the sphere of human relationships ; yet it must be insisted that it holds good in both alike. This truth has nowhere been put better than by Professor H. H. Farmer : "From the human side, we may say that it is essential to man's status as a personal being and to his sense of the significance of his moral life, that he should be called upon to make choices and decisions which make a difference and are not merely play acting . . . that he should be able to refuse to do God's will . . . in such wise that his refusal involves that *pro tanto* God's will is not done. . . . It would seem to be necessary, therefore, that there should be *a world which in some way stands over against both the will of God and the will of the*

[1]Col. iii. 6 ; cf. Eph. v. 6.   [2]1 Thess. ii. 16.

individual, having significance for both as that in and through which co-operation can be attained, and genuine sonship on the part of the latter achieved. Or stating it from the divine side, we might say that . . . God was under necessity to set man in a world which in a sense was as yet uncreated, a world in which the full working out of His will would depend upon the responses and decisions of man. It is confirmation of this that those religious philosophies which have failed to insist on *the world of nature and history as having* significance for, and *a relative independence of, the will of God,* nearly always end in a thoroughly depersonalized conception of man's relationship to God. *Minimize the independence of the world, and nothing can save the independence of man."* [1]

We may put this in other words by saying that in any moral universe consisting of free persons there must be room left for an impersonal law of cause and effect working itself out in a manner relatively independent of the personal and immediate "fiat" of the Divine will. And God must be held to "permit" this for the sake of the safeguarding of human freedom and the development of human personality. This principle ordains that consequences shall always follow acts, and in particular that tragic consequences shall follow certain gross infringements of the laws of God's moral universe. And this surely means that, over against the apparent "sternness" of a God who seems to castigate man with punitive retribution, must be set the fact that there are certain happenings for which God may be said to be responsible, not because He directly wills them, but only because they take place in a universe for which He is ultimately responsible, and which He permits to work itself out according to certain definite laws of cause and effect. This would seem to be the only valid solution of our problem on the basis of a theistic rather than a mechanistic conception of the universe.

Furthermore, this principal of cause and effect, functioning in a sense "independently" of God's immediate will, must hold good even in the spiritual realm, and in the most intimate relations of man with man and man with God.[2] "The wages of sin is death",[3]

---

[1] H. H. Farmer, *The World and God,* p. 69 ; italics mine. The present discussion is, of course, grossly inadequate to the magnitude of the problem, but may serve to indicate the lines along which a solution may be sought. Much the best modern treatment of the problem of Providence is to be found in this book by Professor Farmer.

[2] "The man who sins must get the soul of a sinner. If a man could sin and keep the soul of a saint and the bliss of a saint, that would mean the end of all moral distinctions altogether. It is quite impossible to see how a God of love or any other sort of God can run life on any other terms than this of the strictest consequence. By the realiability of consequence we live and by the discipline of it we learn our errors and find the truth which makes free." H. H. Farmer, in *Reconciliation,* November, 1928, p. 209 f.   [3] Rom. vi. 23.

even though God "desireth not the death of a sinner, but rather that he should turn from his wickedness and live." This spiritual law of cause and effect may be amplified by saying that, not only does sin bring forth punishment, but almost invariably sin also brings forth more sin. The moral universe in which we live is so constituted that when man asserts his independence of God, his right, if he so wills, to live for self alone, then he finds that his way of living tends to call forth a similar way of living in other men.[1] We thus arrive at the paradox, most important for our particular problem, that even that which appears to be Divine punishment for sin—and indeed is, inasmuch as God permits sin to reveal its true nature by reproducing its natural results in men's lives—may often itself have to be called sin. Thus even the punishment of sin, in so far as it may itself be sin, may and often does itself fall under God's condemnation.

Does not this line of thought compel us to modify our pre-conception of a stern and angry God meting out merciless punishment to His sinful subjects ? For the Divine punishment, we have seen, is not to be thought of as something external to the sinning, but is to be found in the tragic fact that the regular consequence of sin is to create its own punitive consequences, which are often themselves sinful. What, then, do we mean when we speak about "punishment" inflicted by an "angry" God ? Simply that God's "anger" against sin is revealed by the fact that He has set us down in the kind of world where His love does not mechanically save us from the consequences of our sin. As Principal James Denney has put it, "The divine punishment is the divine reaction against sin expressing itself through the whole constitution or system of things under which the sinner lives."[2] Thus there seems to be no need to speak about God's "anger" and "punishment" as if they implied direct and personal retaliation by God upon the sinner. A Divine will against sin there certainly is, revealed in the creation of a moral order which inexorably attaches consequences to it. But we must not think of the Divine "anger" as if God, so to speak, personally reacted against the sinner with explosive ire and "took it out of him" in punishment.[3]

This argument may have seemed somewhat abstract and remote from the New Testament, and yet it has a completely adequate

[1] This thought would seem to underlie the saying, "All they that take the sword shall perish by the sword" ; Matt. xxvi. 52.

[2] *The Christian Doctrine of Reconciliation*, p. 203.

[3] "What happens to the sinner is simply due to the fact that a moral universe, created by a moral will, is true to itself and affirms itself steadily to the personality which it is seeking to educate into harmony with itself." (H. H. Farmer, in *Reconciliation*, November, 1928, p. 210.)

New Testament basis in the Pauline doctrine of "wrath", which we must now examine in some detail.[1] In the opening chapter of Romans Paul writes : "The wrath of God is revealed from heaven against all ungodliness and unrighteousness of men."[2] Does this mean that God is "angry" with men in an immediate and personal sense, and therefore brings down upon them vengeance and retribution by a specific and deliberate act of the Divine will ? It has been pointed out that, strangely enough, Paul never uses the verb "to be angry" with God as its subject, though when speaking of "love" he uses not only the noun but the verb.[3] It is curious moreover that, although the word "wrath" occurs in Paul's writings no less than twenty-one times, the expression "wrath of *God*" occurs only three times.[4] Much more often Paul uses the word in a curiously impersonal manner ; frequently he speaks absolutely about "*the* Wrath", almost as if it were a proper noun[5] ; and in one passage in particular[6]—which means literally, "Is God unjust who *brings upon us* the Wrath ?"—he uses it with a verb ($\epsilon\pi\iota\phi\epsilon\rho\epsilon\iota\nu$) which, as Dodd says, suggests that "to Paul 'the Wrath' meant, not a certain feeling or attitude of God towards us, but some process or effect in the realm of objective facts."[7] From all this it seems clear that Paul does not think of God as being actively angry in quite the same immediate and personal sense as he thinks of Him as actively loving. Dodd points out that Paul is here in line with the Psalmists and Prophets : "It would be fair to say that in speaking of wrath and judgment the Prophets and Psalmists have their minds mainly on events, actual or expected, conceived as the inevitable results of sin ; and when they speak of mercy, they are thinking mainly of the personal relation between God and His people. Wrath is the effect of human sin : mercy is not the effect of human goodness, but is inherent in the character of God." Similarly Paul, so far as he retains the idea of "wrath", does so, "not to describe the attitude of God to man, but to describe an inevitable process of cause and effect in a moral universe",[8] that is to say, the principle of retribution, relatively independent of God's immediate volition, which is inherent in such a universe—exactly the position which we had already tentatively reached.

That "wrath" for Paul does mean this working out of the law of cause and effect is suggested most clearly when he writes : "After thy hardness and impenitent heart thou treasurest up for thyself

[1]See an admirable note by C. H. Dodd in his Commentary on *Romans*, in the *Moffatt New Testament Commentary, pp.* 20–4.
[2]Rom. i. 18.
[3]e.g. Eph. ii. 4 ; 2 Thess. ii. 16.
[4]Rom. i. 18 ; Col. iii. 6 ; Eph. v. 6.
[5]Rom. iii. 5 ; v. 9 ; xii. 19 ; xiii. 5 ; 1 Thess. ii. 16.
[6]Rom. iii. 5.
[7]Dodd, op. cit., p. 22.
[8]Dodd, *Romans*, p. 23.

wrath in the day of wrath and revelation of the righteous judgment of God ; who will render to every man according to his works."[1] And the further truth, noted above, that the retribution, though in a sense Divine punishment, may in itself involve sin, appears when Paul, immediately after his reference to the revelation of "the wrath of God", adds the words "wherefore God gave them up in the lusts of their hearts unto uncleanness".[2] It is worth noting here, with reference to our own particular problem, that both the effect of law in general and the punitive action of the civil magistrate in particular are defined as "wrath" ; that is to say, so far as the law is the instrument of God and the civil magistrate His agent, they are so, not as agents of His immediate personal will, but because through both alike the working out of the inexorable principle of retribution is illustrated.[3]

If our argument thus far is valid, it provides a real safeguard against the undue exaggeration of the sterner side of the Divine nature. We may now very briefly apply these general principles in the realms of (a) nature, and (b) history.

(a) First then, is God to be held immediately responsible for the sternness and violence of nature, which, it is suggested, are an indication of certain similar elements in God's own nature ? Must we not take account of the fact that Scripture insists that God is the Creator of heaven and earth, and that in His "marvellous works" His own nature is shown forth ?[4] And it is not only the kindly side of nature which is associated with God ; not only is He the giver of corn and oil and wine, the One who sends down the rain in due season : He is also the Controller of nature on her destructive side. Now Pacifism, it is alleged, ignores this side of nature and the light it throws upon the character and the ways of God. For how cruel and violent nature can be, a world full of creatures evolved through the stern discipline of struggle, a world where earthquake and flood and pestilence deal with those creatures with a frightful and seemingly mechanical relentlessness, a catastrophic world, it sometimes seems, inhabited by combative creatures and governed by an awfully castigating God. What sort of a world is this in which to practice the ethic of absolute love ? Can the God who created it and rules it Himself be a God of absolute love ?

Well, what does Jesus say ? Certainly He accepts nature as reflecting the will of God. The sparrow that falls to the ground and

---

[1]Rom. ii. 5 f.   [2]Rom. i. 24.
[3]Rom. iv. 15 : "What the law produces is the Wrath," i.e. the process of sin followed by retribution. Rom. xiii. 4 : the magistrate is "a divine agent bringing the penalty of Wrath upon the evil-doer".
[4]Cf. for example Ps. cvii.

dies does not do so "without your Father".[1] But the amazing thing is that Jesus uses this to illustrate, not the sternness, but the absolute love of God. To Him there was no contradiction between natural catastrophe and a God of absolute love, surely because He realized, as we all must, that in a moral universe, whose end is to train human personalities to love one another, so far from natural calamity running counter to the governing principle of love, it must be an almost essential part of it. For how should men learn to love one another in any deep way, except in a world where sometimes circumstances so challenge us that we are thrown back on one another's sympathy and protective care ?[2] But it is a very different matter, as we shall see later, to find in the fact of natural calamity, as an element in God's training of us, a justification of violent methods in our own "chastisement" of one another.

It is suggestive to trace, particularly in Scripture, the way in which, as religious ideas develop, men have related natural calamity to the "wrath" of God, and sought from it to draw deductions as to His character. In the most primitive stages thunder and earthquake will be regarded as direct manifestations of the Divine "Mystery", however it be conceived, in its most vindictive and destructive form. Once personification of natural forces takes place, such phenomena are explained as signs of the anger of personal gods. Thus in the earliest strata of the Old Testament the anger of Yahweh is seen in earthquake, pestilence and the like. But often it is still an indiscriminate and irrational anger. "The prophets took up this idea, but rationalized it by teaching that disaster is not an outbreak of irresponsible anger, but an expression of the outraged justice of God. There is no disaster but deserved disaster ; . . . sin is the cause, disaster the effect."[3] In Jesus we reach a stage at which even this comparatively high level of thought is transcended. He clearly teaches that there *may* be disaster which is *not* deserved disaster, and that suffering is not necessarily a sign of the Divine displeasure. "Those eighteen, upon whom the tower in Siloam fell and killed them, think ye that they were offenders above all the men that dwell in Jerusalem ? I tell you, Nay."[4] "His disciples asked Him, saying, Rabbi, who sinned, this man, or his parents, that he should be born blind ? Jesus answered, Neither did this man sin, nor his parents, but that the works of God should be made manifest in him."[5] That

---

[1]Matt. x. 29.

[2]"I do not see that the deeper exercises of love, heroic self-sacrifice, tender protectiveness, mutual helpfulness, could ever begin, much less grow, in a world where there were no final hazard like that of death, and no trouble came to us at all except as a just punishment for our sins." (H. H. Farmer, in *Reconciliation*, November, 1928, p. 209.)

[3]Dodd, *Romans*, p. 22 f.

[4]Luke xiii. 4 f.   [5]John ix. 2 f.

is to say, men may undergo suffering which has no relation whatever
to their deserts : yet once we grasp the aim and end of the Divine
purpose in their lives, we shall see that everything may be compre-
hended within the all-embracing love of God.

Finally, when we say that God is "responsible" for this undeserved suffering, we must do so always remembering that (in line
with the general principles already laid down) there is a sense in
which the world of nature must be thought of as relatively independent over against the immediate will of God. So far as catastrophe is "an act of God" it is not an ethical act, but rather what
might be called a "cosmic" act, for which God is responsible only
in the sense that it takes place within a world created by Him ; and
as such it is no real indication of God's ethical character, and no real
contradiction of His absolute love. Each happening in the world of
nature is not to be ascribed to the direct initiative of God. Rather
may He be thought of as the ground of this whole moral order,
which has been created for His purpose and is eternally being
preserved to carry out His ends.

(b) The same considerations hold good in any attempt to trace
the will of God in history. Nothing, of course, is more characteristic
of the Old Testament than its recognition that in history are to be
found the best illustrations, not only of God's love, but also of His
righteous "wrath". Indeed the Prophets read Israel's history as a
constant disciplining by God of His people. We think of Isaiah's
indictment of Israel's sin in a poem with the refrain, "For all this
His anger is not turned away, but His hand is stretched out still."[1]
Moreover, God uses human instruments to carry out His judgments : "Ho, Assyrian, the rod of mine anger, the staff in whose
hand is mine indignation."[2] "The Lord that saith of Cyrus, He is
my shepherd, and shall perform all my pleasure . . . whose right
hand I have holden, to subdue nations before him."[3] God raises up
enemies to oppress His people, and then, when He has done with
these weapons, He breaks them also and casts them away : "Come,
behold the works of the Lord, what desolations he hath made in the
earth ; he breaketh the bow and cutteth the spear in sunder ; he
burneth the chariots in the fire. Be still, and know that I am God."[4]

What is the Christian Pacifist to say to all this ? Doubtless we
shall point out that, just as in the case of nature, so in that of history
the Hebrew thought naively about the activity of God and the
manifestation of His "wrath". But, even so, as Christians we cannot
acquiesce in any view that bows God out of His own world and
denies that there is a Divine Providence at work in history. We shall

[1]Isa. xix. 12, 17, 21.   [3]Isa. xliv. 28 f.
[2]Isa. x. 5.   [4]Ps. xlvi. 8–10.

also perhaps console ourselves that probably the plainest of all the lessons which the Old Testament teaches us from history is that God works out His purpose through a "remnant", a minority ready to think and act ahead of the community as a whole, and so to keep alive the vision of God's redemptive way. But the argument remains, and must be frankly faced, that history sometimes seems to show war to be a divinely sanctioned way of meeting and overcoming evil. Even if our opponents waive their right of appeal to the "righteous" and "God-approved" wars of the Old Testament, not to speak of modern times, they can still argue that war, though the consequence of human sin, is also the divinely permitted remedy for sin. Measured against the absolute perfection of the ethic of the Kingdom of God war may never be right : but, since man is a fallen creature, it may be relatively right in God's sight, and as such a necessary and legitimate expression of one side of the Divine nature. Have we any answer to this ?

Following the general principles laid down in this chapter, we shall reply that, just as there are elements in the world of nature, so are there elements in the world of history which, if the freedom of human personality is to be safeguarded, must be considered to be relatively independent of the immediate will of God. There thus may be much in history which cannot legitimately be claimed as a revelation either of the will of God or His essential nature. "It is not unimportant to realize", writes Professor Farmer, "that to speak of a general revelation of God in *all* nature and history is . . . almost a contradiction in terms." "The notion that faith should be able to discern the active presence of God in all events and all situations is merely pietistic ; it is neither supported by experience nor necessitated by the thought of God and His intercourse with man."[1] It is true, of course, that nothing can be held to be entirely outside the sphere of Divine Providence, since God cannot be other than the Lord of His world ; but this does not permit us to take any particular line of human activity, either in the past or in the present, and withdraw it from the scope of the principle that human freedom is permitted and retribution follows human sin, as if we were then entitled to say, "This is, or was, the Lord's doing". We are not reduced to a choice between a theory of blind chance and the theory that every separate event must be ascribed to the immediate will of God. There is a third possibility, namely that God does not directly cause the separate events, but that they do all lie within the all-embracing power and wisdom of His providence.

Furthermore, when we recall that the result of sin is commonly to bring forth not only punishment but also more sin, so that sin is

[1] *The World and God*, pp. 85, 90.

chastened by sin, new light falls upon some of the seemingly strange ways of God in history, as for example when He is said to use the ruthless methods of the heathen Cyrus for the punishment of His own people.[1] Here is the "wrath" of God making even evil subserve His purpose, so that "surely the wrath of man shall praise thee".[2] The punishment of sin by sinful men using sinful methods can in this sense be God's punishment, but the methods do not thereby cease to be sinful, nor can God be held to will or to sanction such methods for our imitation. We are, of course, merely groping on the edge of an impenetrable mystery, and we may venture once again to quote Professor Farmer, whose book has been found so helpful in this discussion : "That events should be really the result of the interplay of intramundane causes, including the choices of beings who are free to resist God, and yet also be controlled and directed by His manifold wisdom and sovereign will ; that God has a purpose which He is working out in history . . . yet which, being God's purpose, transcends history altogether so that man cannot interpret it adequately in terms of this life ; that in spite of all the confusion and heartbreak and frustration of life . . . every individual may, if he will, not in imagination but in fact, rest upon a love which numbers the very hairs of his head—that is a conception before which the intellect sinks down to complete paralysis. It is only possible to maintain because in the religious awareness something deeper than intellect is involved."[3]

(2) We are now in a position to answer the second half of our original question. Even granted that there is indeed a "sterner" side to the Divine nature, is it ever competent for the Christian, in his ethical dealings with his fellows, to seek to imitate God on this side of His activity ? Enough has been said to indicate how perilous would be such an assumption. Turning now to the New Testament we may make these preliminary observations :

(a) True to the Old Testament, Jesus evidently regards punitive justice as being specifically a function of God Himself, not to be usurped by man : "Shall not God avenge His elect, which cry to Him day and night, and He is longsuffering over them ?"[4] And Paul strikes exactly the same note : "Avenge not yourselves, beloved, but give place unto wrath (i.e. stand aside and allow God's 'Wrath' to have its way) : for it is written, Vengeance belongeth unto me ; I will recompense, saith the Lord." Then immediately there follows the great Pacifist watchword : "But if thine enemy hunger, feed him ; if he thirst, give him to drink : for in so doing thou shalt heap

[1] Isaiah xliv. 28 f.   [2] Ps. lxxvi. 10.
[3] *The World and God*, p. 100 f. I wish to acknowledge much helpful suggestion, both in this section and the next, from conference with several friends, in particular Prof. Norman W. Porteus, Rev. Oliver Dryer, and Rev. A. C. Craig.
[4] Luke xviii. 7.

coals of fire upon his head. Be not overcome of evil, but overcome evil with good."[1]

(b) Though, as we have seen, Jesus certainly does not close His eyes to the stern side of the Divine nature, yet it is *the other side* which is always held up to men for imitation, if they are to be "sons of the Father", that is to say reflect in their own conduct that which is truly characteristic of God : "Love your enemies, and pray for them that persecute you ; that ye may be sons of your Father which is in heaven : for he maketh his sun to rise on the evil and the good, and sendeth rain on the just and the unjust."[2]

(c) As has been suggested in a previous chapter,[3] in this matter of the right to inflict penalty the gulf between God and man is so great that we cannot regard Divine methods of justice, even when parabolically illustrated from human life by Jesus Himself, as *ipso facto* approved by Jesus for human imitation. We cannot possibly argue from God's way to what ought to be man's way until we have shown that the enormous dissimilarity between God and man makes no difference. Our duty as Christians is not to imitate God, but first to realize God's redemptive purpose towards ourselves, and secondly so to act towards our fellows as to make credible and effective the way of God as revealed in Jesus Christ.

To turn now to more specific questions concerning this suggested "imitation" of God :

(a) If God in nature can use destructive violence and yet remain loving, may not we do so also, even to the extent of war ? Does the fact of natural catastrophe, as an element essential in God's training of us, provide any justification of violent methods in our dealings with one another ? Surely not. For the one justification we were able to find for the unkindliness of the natural world was that it does as a matter of fact teach men to love one another and provide opportunities for mutual help. It may be argued, no doubt, that war does, at least as one of its by-products,[4] have the same noble consequences. But it would be preposterous to claim that generally speaking war educates the human race in love and fellowship and mutual helpfulness. On the contrary it is both the product and the cause of hatred and division and mutual destructiveness. The question appears closed when we remember that natural calamity has been shown to be a "cosmic" rather than an ethical act of God, and that there cannot possibly be any human parallel to such "cosmic" activity.[5]

[1]Rom. xii. 19–21.   [2]Matt. v. 44 f.   [3]See p. 26.   [4]For this see pages 75 f. below.
[5]"Obviously you cannot argue straight away from the Deity making a suitable cosmic setting for the education of the race in love to one or two members of that race dealing with one another. Obviously the fact that One is the Supreme Educator and the others a few of the very immature educatees makes all the difference." (H. H. Farmer, in *Reconciliation*, November, 1928, p. 209.)

(*b*) Because God permits the working out of a moral law of cause and effect in the punishment of sin, must we not, however unwillingly, acquiesce in men suffering for our sins and their own, and indeed consent to play our part in the punishment of those sins ? May not war, for example, be regarded as society co-operating with God in affirming the moral order ? Such an argument seems to me undoubtedly to justify certain restrictive and even forcible social sanctions. Just as God's universe has laws which react against the evil-doer, so must our society have laws which similarly react and similarly demand penalties. Otherwise no moral order of society could exist. But what do we really mean when we speak about "affirming the moral order" ? Presumably we mean "demonstrating it to be what in point of fact it is". And if, as the Christian believes, the moral order is one whose basic principle is love, then only such social sanctions are justifiable as shall result in just such a demonstration ; that is to say, they must be ultimately not merely punitive but "redemptive", designed to win men back from evil to good by evoking from them a response to the appeal of love. Any sanction which in its essential nature contradicts this principle is wrong : and *that is why war is wrong.* We shall never "affirm" to a man that the moral order in which we live is one of love by blowing him in pieces with high-explosive, however clearly we may have first represented to him that our action is the inevitable consequence of his own previous wrong-doing. This line of thought must be more fully developed in the next chapter.

(*c*) Because in history God has apparently used human instruments for the accomplishment of His righteous will, as for example in the case of Cyrus, are we therefore justified in regarding ourselves, and even offering ourselves, as the agents of God's punitive retribution—once again even to the extent of war ? That might seem to be human logic. And yet this is surely just one of those situations in which Paul sometimes felt compelled to call a halt to the arguments of human logic with a "God forbid !"[1] There are some conclusions which it would be a sin against the Gospel of God's love to draw. God Himself may be able to do or "permit" certain things, which men can never do, without stultifying His ultimate aim of redemption, because God is Holy and we are not. And in order to 'affirm the moral order" of love even God had to add to His inexorable law of retribution, and to His human agents for the chastisement of sin, a Saviour who came and bore in His own Person the worst consequences of sin, and broke the vicious circle of cause and effect by leading men to repentance. And that is why— quite apart from the fact that there is in truth no punitive activity

[1] e.g. Rom. iii. 4, 6, 31, etc. ; Gal. ii. 17, etc. I owe this thought to Prof. Porteus.

of God which we *can* imitate, seeing that God's punishment is "Wrath" in the sense already defined, to which there is no possible human parallel—our duty in this connection is not to try to imitate God. Our duty is rather to point men to God's "redemptive" way, and so to act towards our fellows as to make that Divine way credible. The faith of the Christian Pacifist is that war is the greatest of all stumbling-blocks in the way of belief in the credibility and effectiveness of God's redemptive method of overcoming evil, as He has revealed it to us in Jesus Christ, and that the refusal to meet force with force would do more than anything else to make the Gospel credible to a world in bondage to cynicism and fear. We men cannot set ourselves up as petty gods seeking to "imitate" certain mysterious cosmic functions of the Divine activity ; we can imitate the way of Jesus, who, even though it were admitted that He does not fully reflect *all* the attributes of God, does by His teaching and example give us all the guidance necessary for the ordering of our relations with our fellow-men.

CHAPTER SIX

THE LAW, THE GOSPEL, AND THE CROSS

IN the last chapter we dealt with the charge that Christian Pacifism fails to do justice to the sterner side of the Divine nature. A second count in the charge of "heresy" is that Pacifism unduly exalts the Gospel of love at the expense of righteousness and law. Sometimes the charge is made on the ground of an alleged misinterpretation of Scripture, as for example when Dr. Temple accuses Pacifists of the "Marcionite" error of so interpreting the New Testament that it wholly supersedes the Old. But there is a Gospel vein in the Old Testament also. Even as far back as the eighth century we meet Hosea, the prophet of God's love; and as Israel advances towards a truer understanding of God, her thinkers pass beyond the crude "justice" of the books of Joshua and Judges to the profoundly "Christian" standpoint of the book of Jonah: "Doest thou well to be angry? . . . Thou hast had pity on the gourd . . . and should not I have pity on Nineveh, that great city?"[1] On any modern understanding of the relation of the Old Testament to the New, and of the growing revelation of God and His purpose which we have in both, it must surely be admitted that the method of the Law, as set out in the Old Testament, is a noble but an essentially pre-Christian and sub-Christian attempt to point the way to a right relationship between man and God and between man and man, and that in the New Testament there is revealed to us "a more excellent way".[2] It is as *Christians* and not otherwise that we accept the Old Testament as well as the New Testament as God's Word, and we are therefore entitled to take to the interpretation of the Old Testament the insight which has come to us from the New. For this we have sufficient warrant in Jesus' own words, "Ye have heard that it was said to them of old time, . . . : But I say unto you".[3] It is because Jesus Christ came that the Old Testament still makes sense. We have Jesus' warrant, too, for believing in a progressive revelation of God's ways, as men grow in their capacity to understand them, and for the conviction that certain aspects of truth, only implicit even in Jesus' own teaching, are bound to become more and more explicit to the Christian conscience under the guidance of the Holy Spirit: "I have yet many things to say

[1] Jonah iv. 9–11.   [2] 1 Cor. xii. 31.   [3] Matt. v. 21f.

E

unto you, but ye cannot bear them now. Howbeit when he, the Spirit of truth, is come, he shall guide you into all the truth ; . . . for he shall take of mine, and shall declare it unto you."[1]

But the argument usually takes a more theological form ; the Law, it is asserted, must always precede the Gospel, and remain as its indispensable foundation. Again we may quote Dr. Temple : "Sound doctrine and experience alike assure us that the stage of the Law must precede that of the Gospel, and that, though the Gospel carries us far beyond the Law, we need the foundation provided by the Law to be secure before we can truly respond to the Gospel. . . . It was to a people long disciplined by the Law that the Gospel was proclaimed." Just how easily such an argument can be turned to account by the militarist will be seen if we re-write it in militarist terms, as has been done by Professor C. E. Raven, who himself, of course, dissents : "Justice is the essential preliminary to peace ; and justice can be established only on the basis of acknowledged law. In human history Moses preceded Jesus, and it was upon the foundation of legalism that the superstructure of the Gospel was built. We must proceed by the same sequence. The machinery already exists ; and if another generation has to be immolated before it can be set to work, the sacrifice may be inevitable and justified by its results. Let us prepare for another war to end war."[2]

Now Dr. Temple's statement just quoted, though it contains of course a large measure of truth, is also quite dangerously misleading. If he is right in insisting that the Law must always precede the Gospel and must remain as its permanent foundation, then not only must the argument of most of Paul's Epistles go by the board, but the Apostle had no right to presume to proclaim the Gospel to Gentiles without first thoroughly training them under the discipline and the sanctions of the Law. It is the very essence of New Testament teaching that the grace of God in the Gospel is operative towards men who are unrighteous and not yet obedient to the Law's discipline : "God commendeth His own love towards us, in that, *while we were yet sinners*, Christ died for us."[3] It has been the evangelical experience of all the great Christian saints from St. Paul downwards to be reduced to despair just because they could not obey the Law and thus "qualify" for the Gospel ; and it is the experience of all Christian teachers that it is fruitless to try to

[1]John xvi. 12 ff.
[2]C. E. Raven, in *Reconciliation*, March, 1936, p. 60.
[3]Rom. v. 8.

inculcate the Christian ethic before the heart has been changed by the Gospel of the grace of God.[1]

In reply to the charge that Christian Pacifism, by exalting the Gospel of absolute love, dethrones the conception of law and justice taken over by Jesus Himself from the Old Testament "Law" and "Prophets", and thereby undermines the very foundations of righteousness, we may now note the following points in greater detail :

(1) Jesus' new and distinctive ethic, *and in particular the definitely pacifist features in it*, is specifically stated by Himself to have as its aim not the "destruction" but the "fulfilment" of the Law. The whole section begins with the statement : "Think not that I came to destroy the law or the prophets : I came not to destroy, but to fulfil."[2] And at the end of the section we have the "non-resistance" and "love-your-enemy" sayings as the culminating illustrations of what Jesus means by "fulfilling the law". To "fulfil the law" in Jesus' thought evidently means to "give the full content" to the older conception of Law, "to draw out its underlying intention", "to make explicit that which hitherto has been only implicit". Just how His pacifist ethic achieves this we shall discuss in a moment. Meantime it is important to note that Jesus Himself, though definitely claiming to modify and in a sense even to supersede the Law, just as definitely denies that He is "destroying" it.

Paul, too, frankly admits that in large measure the Gospel, when rightly understood, has superseded the Law—but always in the sense not of "destroying" the Law, but of accomplishing that at which the Law aimed, but failed to achieve.[3] We are guilty of "heresy", not when with Paul himself we recognize and insist upon this kind of supersession of the Law by the Gospel, but when like Marcion and Dr. Temple himself we set the way of justice and the way of love in so sharp an antithesis as to suggest that when we choose the one we necessarily "destroy" the other. Neither Jesus' teaching nor Paul's means that justice has been dethroned by love ; it does mean that all human relationships must ultimately be based on the Gospel of love ; that justice truly "fulfilled" is an outcome of love, rather than love a mere by-product of justice ; that if we aim at love we shall establish justice by the way ; that we can in

---

[1]"The Gospel is not a postcript to Christian ethics, but their presupposition and preface ; the love of God in the Gospel precedes the righteousness which makes it possible, and not *vice versa*. . . . If the foundation of Law had to be secure before we can truly respond to the Gospel, Christianity is a fair-weather religion, and its distinctive ethics cannot get started at all until it is no longer needed. If you must not begin to love your enemies until there are none, Christ's command is rendered meaningless." (J. S. Whale, in *Reconciliation*, April, 1936, p. 93.)

[2]Matt. v. 17.

[3]*Romans* throughout, especially Chapters VII and VIII.

fact secure justice only when we aim primarily not at it, but at the love out of which it springs. Paul feels the same about peace : like love it is one of the "fruits of the Spirit",[1] the reward of a whole way of life, to be attained not by aiming at "peace" alone, but as one of the "by-products of a larger quest".[2]

(2) Before we ask how the pacifist ethic of Jesus does actually thus "fulfil" or, to use more modern language, "sublimate" the conception of law and righteousness, it will be well to recall what was said above[3] about "affirming the moral order". Jesus does not think, as do we too often with our academic ways of thought, of a "moral order" in the abstract, which evil, again in the abstract, has invaded, and which has to be "vindicated" by resistance to evil as a thing *per se*. That is to use legal and political analogies, and results in the misconception that God is concerned with abstract "law" rather than with persons, and that His chief end is to "vindicate the moral order of the universe", and to "uphold His own righteousness", rather than to fulfil His purpose of redemption towards mankind. Jesus on the other hand is dealing always, not with such an abstract "moral order", but with a world consisting of persons in relation to one another and to God ; and in such a world justice can truly be "vindicated", and God's own righteousness "upheld", not by the mere restraint and punishment of evil, but only by making evil persons see the sinfulness of their ways,[4] through the employment of a redemptive method which will change the evil will, and restore right personal relationships, "so making peace".[5] For peace in the international sphere also depends upon something much more than the restraining of an "agressor" or the vindication of a "righteous cause". Peace depends upon right relations between persons, upon mutual confidence in the common honesty, upon co-operation by all for the service of all, upon

[1]Gal. v. 22.

[2]The phrase is Raven's : *Reconciliation*, March, 1936, p. 61.

[3]P. 63.

[4]The common fallacy here in much of our thinking is that "the moral order, as inherent in the divine justice, appears as something standing over against the individual's inner life, capable of affirming itself and achieving its sovereign rights whether the inner life is redeemed or not." "But what if the moral order be, in the last analysis, nowhere save in the purposes and volitions of persons in relation to one another ? In that case only in so far as those purposes and volitions are not merely checked and defeated, but also recreated into what they ought to be, can the moral order be said to be victorious in any sense that really matters. For only then will it have reaffirmed itself at the precise point where it has been negated and denied. We affirm then, that a moral order which merely checks and annuls is not one which has at the heart of it an absolute valuation of the individual person as such ; it is not the sort of moral order which is known to the Christian in and through his reconciliation to God through Christ." (H. H. Farmer, *The World and God*, pp. 252, 249 f.)

[5]Eph. ii. 15.

something far deeper than mere justice in the abstract, however ingeniously worked out by international "formulae". There can be no peace in any sphere at all which is not also what Paul calls "the peace of God which surpasses all human ingenuity".[1]

(3) How, then, does Jesus' pacifist ethic redeem the will from evil to good, restore right personal relationships, and thus truly "fulfil" and sublimate the Law ? It does so because it offers, not merely negative passivity in the face of wrong, but an alternative, positive, and redemptive method of overcoming evil, which renders all violent and punitive methods obsolete. The injunction to non-resistance,[2] which is so often taken to represent the whole pacifist ethic, is immediately followed by the positive commandment of all-embracing love. Retributive justice, which merely checks and punishes evil, is supplanted by active and self-sacrificial love, which redeems and changes the evil will, so "vindicating righteousness" in the only true sense of the word, and thereby "fulfilling the Law". This, and not mere non-resistance, must always be the foundation of the Pacifist position when adopted on specifically Christian grounds. For the Christian, if he renounces war, will do so, not because he denies that to react against evil by way of war may sometimes be better than not to react at all, but because he is convinced that to use such methods is equivalent to trying to cast out devils by Beelzebub the prince of devils,[3] and must stultify at the outset every effort to make credible and effective this alternative and positive method of sacrificial and redemptive love, to which as a disciple of the Crucified he is called.

It is unnecessary to repeat here what was said in Chapter Three about how Jesus in His own Person and by His own example proved again and again the power of active love to overcome the evil in men's lives. And in the Cross the method of non-resistance finds its complete and final illustration, and the redemptive way of sacrificial love its perfect example. For Jesus deliberately willed to endure the Cross rather than prove false to His chosen redemptive way, believing that He and His could overcome the evil in men only by being willing to suffer to the uttermost rather than betray that way ; and at Calvary we see Him laying down life rather than take it, in His own Person meeting the wickedness of violent men, Himself bearing sin's utmost penalty, the Just for the unjust, and yet over-coming that sin by the power of active, forgiving love. It is important, too, to remember that Jesus never sought to avoid the application of these principles because that way might lead to suffering and danger for others as well as for Himself. He never

---

[1]Phil. iv. 7 : again the phrase is Raven's ; *Reconciliation*, March, 1936, p. 61.
[2]Matt. v. 39.   [3]Matt. xii. 24.

promised immunity even from death itself to those who accepted His way : "If any man would come after me, let him . . . take up his cross, and follow me."[1] When He "stedfastly set His face to go to Jerusalem",[2] He risked His followers' lives as well as His own. If He had been swayed by considerations of their safety, there would have been no Cross. But there would also have been no Resurrection, and no releasing into the world of the redemptive power of love.

What is it that gives to the Cross, and to the whole way of life of which it is the symbol, this unique "redemptive" power, that is the power to defeat evil by changing the evil will and winning it to good ? I know of no finer statement than this : "God's purpose is to win men's hearts to Himself. . . . Obviously there is only one method of winning such a victory when methods of force are ruled out, and that is simply to love ; to love so passionately, so utterly, that even the most brutal and seemingly triumphant violence of sin leaves it still love, unchanged except in the increasing agony of its disappointed desire to bless and to redeem. The only qualification for victory required of love is that it should be able to endure its most shattering defeat and yet still remain love. If it does that, it has still got the whip hand ; for in its very weakness of defeat it has within it the invincible strength of remaining itself, and it will yet win its victory. As someone has said, 'You cannot defeat defeat'. . . . Let men take every advantage of the seeming weakness of love, let them bruise and batter and seek utterly to smash it, as they did at the Cross ; but let it still remain love, and in the end they will have to give up, and look upon what their hands have done, and break down in its presence. At some time or other the very weakness of love will cut them to the centre of their being with more power than a two-edged sword—only it will be spiritual power. I am sure that is so, human hearts being what they are. The weakness of a God of love is stronger than men."[3]

We shall no doubt be met with the rejoinder that only a sentimentalist would dream of trying to apply the method of redemptive love to international affairs. This is what Dr. Temple apparently has in mind when he accuses Pacifists of a "Pelagian" heresy. "Man," he writes,[4] "is incapable of living by love unless the grace of God has both converted and sanctified him ; so that the law of love is not applicable to nations consisting in large measure of unconverted or (as is the case of most, if not all, of us) very imperfectly converted citizens." We would prefer to believe that Dr. Temple merely means that the perfectly converted alone can

[1]Mark viii. 34.
[2]Luke ix. 51.

[3]H. H. Farmer, *Things not Seen*, p. 32 f.
[4]*York Diocesan Leaflet*, 1935.

love perfectly, and not, as might appear at first sight, that the way of love can be effective only when directed towards the perfectly converted. For to say that love has a saving and redeeming power only when directed towards the wholly converted and sanctified is surely a denial of the whole of the New Testament. If the last part of Dr. Temple's statement is true in that sense, then both Jesus and Paul were manifestly sadly at fault. The Jews were a very imperfectly converted nation in Jesus' own day, yet "God so loved the world that he gave his only Son,"[1] and Jesus so loved His people that He died for them at Calvary. Was His Cross after all inapplicable ? Was Paul merely presumptuous when he preached "a more excellent way"[2] to folk at Corinth who were still heathen ? Was he deceiving himself when he wrote "God commendeth his own love towards us, in that, *while we were yet sinners*, Christ died for us" ?[2] But, taking Dr. Temple's words as they stand, his inference apparently is that in matters affecting the relations of nation with nation the Church must be content to fall into line with the State in reverting to a sub-Christian ethic. A more legitimate inference would surely be that the Church must refuse to collaborate with the State in so far as the State still finds itself unable or unwilling to apply an ethic which is binding on the Church. "Love is not applicable to nations," says Dr. Temple, "therefore Christians, when they act as members of their nations, are not bound by the law of love." "No !" replies the Christian Pacifist, "if nations cannot or will not act as Christians should, then Christians cannot conform to what the nation does." If this alternative is, as Dr. Temple asserts, "heresy", many of us would insist that his own alternative is just as surely "apostasy".

The third and last count in the charge of heresy is that the line of thought which we have been following misinterprets the true significance of the Cross, and this in three ways :

(1) First, it is alleged, the Christian Pacifist ignores the fact that the Cross is *theologically unique*. "Our Lord's death upon the Cross had relations and meanings to which nothing in our life corresponds. He died on the Cross as the World's Redeemer. This is the great message of the New Testament regarding His death."[4] Though in large measure true, such a statement is just as perilous as are all half-truths. Similarly, it might be argued with much truth that Jesus, as only Son of God, had a sense of vocation also entirely unique, and a redemptive aim and purpose with which that of even the noblest of His martyr followers is in no wise comparable. This is the whole force of such sayings as, "Christ also suffered for sins

---

[1]John iii. 16.   [2]1 Cor. xii. 31.   [3]Rom. v. 8.
[4]Isaac Jolly, *Pacifism at the Bar of Holy Scripture and History*, p. 18.

once, the righteous for the unrighteous, that he might bring us to God",[1] or, "we have been sanctified through the offering of the body of Jesus Christ *once for all*".[2] This is a sacrifice never to be repeated and never emulated. Moreover, we are reminded, Jesus Himself seems to have fully realized that there was something unique in the setting of His self-sacrifice both in time and in place. Hence the constant references to "His hour".[3] "It is to be recognized that there was a place and a time which alone would suit the purpose of His suffering, so that man might understand it and take it to his heart and conscience. Other hands would inflict it, but only when He chose to exercise His determining power to give or to withhold. The narratives make it plain that Simon Peter's public recognition furnished a signal that His hour was at hand, since the Church's foundation of faith confessed had at last been laid as a living rock. Till the hour came which alone accorded with the fulfilment and secure recognition of His redemptive aim He had withdrawn, again and again, from the grasp of His enemies, thus plainly showing that suffering and death were not of themselves sufficient apart from adequate recognition. But in Jerusalem, at a Passover season, in full view alike of disciples, people and rulers, He found His hour and His altar, and as a Lamb suffered Himself to be led to the Sacrifice, a Paschal offering, a Ransom for many."[4] Jesus' unique redemptive purpose, the choice—not to say predestined appointment—of both time and place, gives His sacrifice a redemptive efficacy which does not in any comparable manner belong to the "method of sacrificial love", when adopted by His disciples as a professed and regular manner of life.

Now all this is admittedly and gloriously true. And yet the manner chosen by Jesus to fulfil His redemptive purpose must surely have been in line with His whole daily manner of life, and must have owed its efficacy precisely to that consistency. His final victory over evil on the Cross cannot have been by means inconsistent with those by which He won daily victories over evil in the men and women with whom He came into contact. His triumph over sin cannot have been won by a method out of harmony and incomparable with that method by which He bade His disciples overcome evil when they met it in their fellows. In other words, to amend our previous quotation : "Our Lord's death on the Cross had relations and meanings to which *a very great deal in our life*

[1] i Pet. iii. 18.

[2] Heb. x. 10.

[3] This is, of course, chiefly in the Fourth Gospel, and may perhaps be held to reflect the point of view rather of the Apostolic Church than of Jesus Himself. See John ii. 4 ; vii. 30 ; viii. 20 ; xii. 23 ; xii. 27 ; xiii. 1 ; xvii. 1.

[4] I owe this fine statement to my friend Principal W. A. Curtis.

corresponds." Paul himself, though he constantly emphasizes the uniqueness of Christ's sacrifice, insists, too, that the Christian must be "crucified with Christ", if the Cross of Calvary is to have any efficacy for him.[1]

Moreover if it be true, as we believe it is, that Jesus throughout His whole ministry was seeking "a place and a time which alone would suit the purpose of His suffering" ; if it be true that it was the hour of the Cross which "accorded with the fulfilment and secure recognition of His redemptive aim" ; and if it is these truths which give to the Cross its peculiar characteristics and its redemptive quality—then it must also be true that the Cross was the goal towards which Jesus' purpose more and more consciously moved throughout His entire ministry. And if the Cross had this central place in Jesus' whole Messianic consciousness, then we have no right to isolate it as a theological mystery which has no bearing on the ethic which He taught or the personal decisions which He made. Indeed we seem to be driven back to our previous conclusion that Jesus, knowing Himself to be Messiah, knowing also what popular expectation demandeth of Messiah, yet living always with His face set towards Calvary, must have seen in the Cross the direct Divine alternative to the eagerly awaited Messianic war.

(2) Secondly, we are told that Pacifists forget that the Cross is *ethically not for our imitation.* "Jesus, in His death on the Cross, is not in the New Testament held up chiefly as an example for our imitation, but as the object of our faith. We are not chiefly called upon to imitate Him, but to trust Him as Saviour."[2] That is to say, Jesus, who discriminated so carefully in the occasion for His own sacrifice, left no example or rule to be followed blindly or without discrimination. Again this is in so large a measure true, and yet such a dangerous half-truth. Paradoxical surely, that our critics should be so ready for us to imitate the transcendent God in His cosmic "wrath", and so loath that we should imitate the Cross of God incarnate in the Man Jesus ! There is a sense in which, none would deny, Jesus' redemptive sacrifice once for all for the world's sin need not and cannot be repeated. Yet, whatever be true of the New Testament as a whole, Jesus Himself *does* hold up the Cross for His disciples' imitation. There is no word of Jesus more often repeated in the Gospels than that in which He bids them follow Him along the road to the Cross.[3] Even if He was speaking only in metaphor, He could not have done so had He not seen in the way of life He set before them something in common with His own supreme sacrifice. And such a passage as the following shows that

[1] Gal. ii. 20 ; v. 24.   [2] Isaac Jolly, op. cit., p. 18.
[3] Matt. x. 38 ; xvi. 24 ; Mark viii. 34 ; x. 31 ; Luke ix. 23 ; xiv. 27.

the early Church realized that Jesus did so call upon His disciples to follow Him : "For hereunto were ye called : because Christ also suffered for you, leaving you an example, that ye should follow his steps . . . who his own self bare our sins in his body upon the tree."[1]

This particular objection to the Pacifist position is perhaps due to a wrong idea of what "imitation of the Cross" implies. The Pacifist is sometimes accused of regarding the Cross as a mechanical device whose efficacy depends on the power of self-sacrifice *per se*, and then of arrogantly presuming to "imitate the Cross" under the misconception that any such isolated and indiscriminate act of self-sacrifice will have a similar automatic redemptive power. But the Christian Pacifist position is exactly the reverse. Always it is not suffering as such that redeems, but the readiness to accept suffering rather than deny the Truth, obedience to a particular way of life with self-sacrifice, if necessary, as a possible climax. For Jesus the Cross meant risking everything on His conviction that God's way of overcoming evil would work. Therefore we see in the Cross, not a mechanical act of self-sacrifice which Jesus imagined would be effective *ex opere operato*, but the inevitable climax, under the conditions which confronted Him, to a consistent life-practice of meeting evil not by violence, not even by involing law, but by the way of forgiving and reconciling love. Jesus died rather than betray that love method. So in our own problem : if there are circumstances in which there seems no alternative to self-sacrifice, it is precisely because any other alternative would be a betrayal of the specifically Christian method of overcoming evil by redemptive love. By "imitating the Cross" we mean, not presumption in martyrdom, but loyalty to the life-practice of redemptive love with its possible climax in a cross, that is to say a way of life which as a last resort is willing to sacrifice itself rather than betray itself.

So in our international problem. A nation, following the way of Christ, might feel called upon to adopt a policy of total disarmament. But it would do so, in the first instance, not with the deliberate purpose of courting martyrdom, but with the conviction that the best safety from the perils against which nations arm is to be found in a new national way of life, which would remove causes of provocation and lead progressively to reconciliation and peace. It, too, would risk everything on the conviction that God's way would work. But such a nation must also be willing, if necessary, to incur the risk of national martyrdom by refusing to equip itself against the possibility of aggression. And it may be that the world must wait for its redemption from warfare until one nation is ready to risk crucifixion at the hands of its possible enemies. It might lose

[1] Pet. ii. 21 f.

its own national life ; but it would set free such a flood of spiritual
life as would save the world. To many of us this may not be a very
welcome or comforting implication to discover in the Cross. Yet it
may be well to remind ourselves that no interpretation of the Cross
is likely to be a true one which is not to-day, as of old, an "offence"
to the "Jew", and to all who like him are obsessed with "law" and
"righteousness", and "folly" to the politically minded "Greek".
The Pacifist interpretation of the Cross is certainly both. It may
once again prove to be "the power of God, and the wisdom of
God".[1]

(3) Lastly Pacifists are accused of unjustifiably narrowing the
idea of "redemption", and appropriating the word "redemptive"
to their own peculiar way of life. May it not be possible, we are
asked, in a war waged on behalf of righteousness, for the soldier
himself to become the embodiment of redemptive sacrifice, facing
as he does at the call of duty and for love of a cause suffering,
mutilation and death ? And is there not a certain arrogance in
claiming the title "redemptive", as if it were applicable only to the
love which refuses to take part in warfare, because it believes that
it knows a more excellent way, and refusing it to the love which
lays down life on the battlefield in conflict with evil militant,
because it chooses the highest way it knows and believes that love
has nothing more to give ? "Greater love hath no man than this,
that a man lay down his life for his friends."[2] This is a fair question
and must be frankly faced. Let it be sadly confessed that spiritual
pride is apt to be the besetting temptation, if not the besetting sin,
of Pacifists. And let it be humbly and gratefully acknowledged that
such self-sacrifice on the battlefield for pure and unselfish ends may
be the symbol of a love than which no man has a greater ; let us
even admit that in a broad sense it may be "redemptive". But it is
clearly not "redemptive" in the particular sense in which we have
been using the word. For we have been discussing two alternative
methods or lines of action for the meeting and overcoming of evil ;
by "redemptive" we mean "possessing the power to win over the
will from evil to good" ; and the word has been used throughout
our discussion in the more specific sense of "redemptive" of that
particular evil against which action is being directed, in this case
what we have just called "evil militant" in the person of my enemy.
Now let me assume (per impossible, it is to be feared) that my cause
in battle is wholly right and my enemy's wholly wrong. Even so,
will my self-sacrifice in opposition to him on the battlefield have
any "redemptive" effect on the evil aggressive will of the enemy
whom I am fighting ? Possibly yes, if my main purpose on the

[1] 1 Cor. i. 23.   [2] John xv. 13.

battlefield was to "lay down my life" as a challenge to and protest against aggressive wickedness. However fantastic may be the idea of a "peace army" deliberately sacrificing itself between the lines, it is quite possible that its sacrifice might have some such moral effect on the spirit of aggression. But the soldier's main purpose in going into battle is not "to lay down his life for his friends". If while on active service he showed the slightest trace of such a desire for simple martyrdom, he would promptly be disciplined. He may be heroically willing to lay down his life ; but his main purpose, the reason for which he has been enlisted, trained, sent to the front, is to win victory, and to do so by killing and wounding as many of the enemy as possible. It is not pleasant to have to make such statements, but the subject is far too serious to admit of any sentimentality. Now what I have to ask is whether *that* line of action on my part—not laying down my own life, but seeking to take his— can possibly have any "redemptive" efficacy, in the sense already defined, with respect to the particular evil against which it is directed, that is to say, the enemy I am seeking to kill. Even supposing that I am wholly right, and he is wholly wrong, can I possibly expect to "redeem" my enemy, win over his will from evil to good, by doing my utmost to kill him ? It needs little knowledge of psychology to suggest that the result is certain to be the very opposite. And, however glorious the by-products of war in duty and courage and self-sacrifice, as realists we know that the soldier is on the battlefield to kill. It would seem that the apologist for war must be far more explicit in his definitions, when he claims to find, even in the by-products of such activity, something which is "redemptive" in the same sense as is the Cross of Jesus Christ.

Our study has seemed to prove that an essential element in the "Gospel" of Jesus Christ is that distinctive method of meeting and overcoming evil, which He set forth in His teaching and illustrated supremely in the Cross. By His words, His life, His death, He demonstrated the power of active and, if need be, sacrificial love to conquer evil, vindicate the moral order, and redeem the will from evil to good. In a word, He overcame evil with good. It is impossible to see how one can eliminate this from the Gospel without changing its whole character, or exempt the Christian from a like obligation without dismissing him forthwith from discipleship. The principle that one cannot cast out devils by the prince of devils is not a matter of opinion to be proved or disproved by cleverly manipulating texts : it lies at the very heart of the Christian ethic as proclaimed and lived by Jesus Christ Himself. He knew no other way of overcoming evil than by redeeming the evil will. Nor will the Christian willingly employ any methods which are not ultimately redemptive. And here surely we have the canon by which we are to judge whether this or that particular use of force can be brought within the orbit of the Christian ethic, the test by failure to pass which war is seen to be under a final prohibition. It comes under the ban mainly for two reasons : firstly, because there is in war as such no single element which is truly redemptive; and secondly, because it results in a complete prostitution of those personal values, and a complete rupture of those personal relationships, apart from which both the Fatherhood of God and the Brotherhood of man are reduced to a mere mockery. It is on this ground of the violation of human personality more than on any other ground that the Christian ethic must renounce war.

Perhaps we may state the case thus : Reconciliation and redemption, which are the supreme ends of the Christian love which is itself the essence of Christian living, can never be achieved by force pure and simple ; for force in itself is much more likely to thwart than to fulfil these ends. If then force is to find a place within the Christian ethic, it must only be in a form which is limited by such sympathetic discrimination that it may be expected to prepare the way for the final appeal of redemptive love. Any use of force, therefore, which by its very nature escapes from such control, and renders such an appeal abortive, can under no circumstances be countenanced. It is obvious that war utterly fails to pass this test, and for these reasons : Firstly, no sooner has war begun than there automatically follows the prostitution of every conceivable moral value, truth, honesty, decency, upon which all stable personal relationships, and the only possibility of recovering them when lost, depend. Secondly, war has, particularly in its modern form, become so entirely mechanical and impersonal that one can engage in it only by totally depersonalizing one's entire relationship to the object of one's action.[1] And thirdly, its main aim is to kill, and

---

[1]Attempts are sometimes made actually to defend modern warfare on the ground that it has become so impersonal : there need be no personal hatred of foe for foe ; each is a machine destroying an unseen enemy, and often not even knowing whether he does so. Yet personality is the watchword of Christian theology ; and right personal relationship is the key to Christian ethics. A true understanding of the mind of Jesus would suggest that there can be few actions more un-Christlike than thus to depersonalize one's attitude to one's brother man. "War represents an anti-personalistic force which regards human personalities as so much cannon fodder, as material to be used for developing the power of the State. There was after all something personal in the idea of the warlike knight—it involved personal valour. Modern war is completely devoid of this element. Armaments and preparations for war, which serve to undermine the very states which adopt these means for the sake of greater power and emancipation, constitute precisely the forces which depersonalize and dehumanize man. This state of things is quite intolerable to the Christian conscience." (Nicolas Berdyaev, in *Reconciliation*, August, 1936, p. 207.)

therefore to remove the presumed object of redemption entirely from that sphere of personal relationship wherein alone love can make its appeal. "War, in short, of necessity, and its essential idea, is a use of force which, from the angle of the demands of love, is a hideous cul-de-sac in personal relations"[1]—a cul-de-sac surely up which no Christian can venture to go.

[1] H. H. Farmer, in *The Christian and War*, p. 6.

CHAPTER SEVEN

CHRIST AND CAESAR

WE have already remarked that neither the teaching of Jesus Himself nor the New Testament as a whole throws very much direct light upon the duty of the Christian citizen towards the State of which he is a member ; and we have touched on one of the chief reasons for this fact.[1] One is inclined to regret this silence all the more because it appears inevitable that the claims of Christianity and of the State, of God and of Caesar, should constantly be coming into conflict, and this for several reasons. Christianity, whose end and goal is the Kingdom of God, has its eyes fixed and its affection set upon things unseen and eternal : the State is inevitably concerned with worldly power and temporal ends. Christianity is a universal religion, knowing no national preference : the State in practice serves exclusively the interests of its own people. Christianity, as the life of the spirit, has its vital breath in freedom : the State has always found it necessary to find its ultimate sanction in coercion and force. Christianity ascribes to human personality an absolute value and independence of all that is of the earth. The State by its claim to ultimate loyalty is compelled to deny this priority and supremacy of the personal. "For the ancients a man was primarily a citizen of his State, first a member of a community and only afterwards a personality. If Christianity has done anything new for political science and jurisprudence, it has been to reverse this order."[2] To-day we have seen the tragic results of the pendulum swinging once again to the opposite extreme.

Hence the dilemma of the Christian Pacifist. He may be first a Christian, but he is also one of the units which compose the community. Can he accept the privileges, and at the same time contract out of the obligations, which are due to his membership of the group ? Must not the individual conscience be subordinate to the common judgment ? When the State goes to war, must not the citizen, whatever his convictions as a Christian, acquiesce and co-operate ? Must not personal responsibility be merged in civic solidarity ? The Christian citizen is confronted by the sorest conflict of loyalties. "As the history both of Christendom and of Christians shows, the adjustment of the claims of these conflicting interests is

[1]See above, p. 45.　　[2]Scholten, quoted by Heering, op. cit. p. 172.

79

a matter of the most acute difficulty. A freedom of conscience which shall escape moral anarchy, an obedience to State authority which stops short of acquiescence in evil, represents an ideal hard to define or sustain."[1]

The tension has become still more acute with the growth of the "Totalitarian State", which has thus been admirably defined by J. H. Oldham : "The totalitarian state is a state which lays claim to man in the totality of his being ; which declares its own authority to be the source of all authority ; which refuses to recognize the independence in their own sphere of religion, culture, education and the family ; which seeks to impose on all its citizens a particular philosophy of life ; and which sets out to create by means of all the agencies of public information and education a particular type of man in accordance with its own understanding of the meaning and end of man's existence." As Mussolini himself has put it : "Fascism conceives of the State as an absolute, in comparison with which all individuals and groups are relative, only to be conceived of in their relation to the State. . . . Nothing against the State; nothing outside the State ; everything for the State." Now it is clear that a State which advances such claims is in fact declaring itself to be also a substitute for an authoritarian Church, and is advancing a view of life which is to be accepted, if not as an actual substitute for religion, then at least as its powerful rival. "Underlying the claims of the Totalitarian State are certain ultimate beliefs regarding the nature and destiny of man. In so far as these are incompatible with the Christian understanding of the meaning and purpose of man's existence, the Church must inevitably be involved in a life and death struggle for its existence. . . . It is clear that between the view that the racial and national soul is the ultimate measure of all values, and the view that all souls, individual and national, are judged by the Gospel, there is an irreconcilable conflict."[2] Nor need we delude ourselves into believing that the danger is confined to countries under authoritarian rule. It is present also in Democratic States so far as such States are swayed by the doctrine of the sovereign authority of the State, a doctrine which really puts the State in the position of God, with complete control over the lives and liberties of its subjects, which it may use as it thinks fit for its own purely selfish and national ends. And there are few if any States which are not so swayed. When the threat is perfectly obvious, as in Germany yesterday and Russia to-day, the only answer may be martyrdom, and through martyrdom comes a new life. The danger is much more subtle when Christian people are unaware that their principles are

[1]C. E. Raven, *Is War Obsolete ?* p. 65.
[2]See J. H. Oldham, *Church, Community and State*, pp. 9-12.

being undermined by the gradual paganizing of the mind of the whole community. The new absolutism of the State is a warning signal of dangers which confront the whole Christian Church. For it is diametrically opposed to the basic principle of the Christian ethic, namely the sovereignty of human personality. "Above all else our epoch stands in desperate need of learning to prize man more highly, of acknowledging the value of every man, even of the least, because every single man bears within himself the image and likeness of God. For this reason one can never regard man as a means to an end, or turn him into a tool in the hands of the State, so as to aid its expansion, or encourage its desire for national self-glorification. Such at least is the Christian point of view. For Christianity man stands far higher than the State and is far more precious than the State : he is unique, an unrepeatable personality."[1]

G. J. Heering has suggested that one of the chief reasons for the failure of historical Christianity to uphold the full Christian ethic in the face of a State which still claims the right to enlist the support of the Church for war is "the suppression of primitive Christian values and the false exegesis of the New Testament concurrent with it".[2] An examination of our problem in the light both of the New Testament passages and of its treatment down the Christian centuries will show just how true this statement is.

Turning then, first to Scripture, we find that the claims of the State are in the main based on two New Testament passages :

Firstly there is Jesus' famous answer to the question whether or no He considered it to be lawful to pay tribute to Caesar : "Render unto Caesar the things that are Caesar's, and unto God the things that are God's."[3] This saying is not seldom used as if it meant that according to Jesus the Christian must not allow religious scruples to interfere with his duty to the State. Such a misplacing of the whole emphasis of Jesus' words is possible only if we completely ignore the context. It is worth reminding ourselves :

(a) The "Caesar" in question is not the government which a patriotic Jew would recognize as having the right to claim his allegiance. He is the representative of a foreign State holding down a conquered people by force of arms. If the saying may be used at all to sanction an unconditional claim by the State upon its subjects, then the duty indicated is not that of taking arms in defence of one's own country's freedom, but the duty of submission to an undesired dictatorship.

[1] Nicolas Berdyaev, in *Reconciliation*, August, 1936, p. 207.
[2] Heering, *The Fall of Christianity*, p. 218. I am particularly indebted to this book for much in this chapter.
[3] Mark xii. 17.

F

(b) The whole point of Jesus' answer is that it enabled Him to escape the trap prepared for Him by the Pharisees, who wished to force Him either to damage His reputation in the eyes of His own people by advocating submission to Rome, or to compromise Himself with the government by advocating resistance. According to ancient ideas Caesar's "image and superscription" on a coin indicated that it was his own property. Well, then, says Jesus, it is surely fair enough to give back to Caesar what is already his own : but see that you likewise pay your debts to God. So far from providing us with a proof-text in support of war, the words are really a Pacifist's disavowal of the policy of violent resistance to an oppressor.

(c) The words have sometimes been turned into an actual apology for war. Thus Augustine, who was one of the first Christian theologians to try to harmonize war with the New Testament, comments : "For indeed tribute is brought with the very object of giving wages to the soldiers, who are indispensable, just because of the wars."[1] But, quite apart from the fact that there is no reference either explicit or implicit to war, the impression left by the passage as a whole is that all the emphasis falls on the second clause, "and render to God the things that are God's". An excellent comment is that of the well-known French scholar Loisy (again no Pacifist) : "Jesus emphasizes the lawfulness of political power and of tribute much less than the insignificance of these things in comparison with the Kingdom of heaven. . . . Let the things of this world be esteemed according to the smallness of their value, and let these duties be discharged as there is necessity ; but let men know above all that the greatest things lie elsewhere, in fidelity to the heavenly Father. It would be to falsify the thought of Jesus to suppose that the debt to Caesar is on the same plane, or that it has the same absolute and definite character, as the duty towards God."[2] At most Jesus suggests that civil obedience need not necessarily clash with the obedience due to God, provided that the claims of the State do not invade the sphere of duty owed to God.

(d) Even such a partial gesture of acquiescence in the claims of the State loses much of its force when we remember that Jesus' view of the Kingdom of God implied that the rule of Rome was doomed to destruction, and that it would be overthrown not by man's agency but by God's. Why then quibble over so small a matter as the payment of taxes ? The head of Caesar on the coin stamps it as his own. Well, then, give him his own, for the time being. But the matter of real importance is your loyalty to God !

But the crowning proof-text of a militarist theology, and the

[1] *Contra Faustum*, xxii. 74.   [2] Loisy, *Les Evangiles Synoptiques*, Vol. II, p. 336.

basis of the whole traditional dogma concerning the relation of
Church to State, has always been Paul's apology for the "higher
powers", which must be quoted in full : "Let every soul be in
subjection to the higher powers : for there is no power but of God ;
and the powers that be are ordained of God. Therefore he that
resisteth the power, withstandeth the ordinance of God : and they
that withstand shall receive to themselves judgment. For rulers are
not a terror to the good work, but to the evil. And wouldst thou
have no fear of the power ? do that which is good, and thou shalt
have praise from the same : for he is a minister of God to thee for
good. But if thou do that which is evil, be afraid ; for he beareth
not the sword in vain : for he is a minister of God, an avenger for
wrath to him that doeth evil. Wherefore ye must needs be in subjection, not only because of the wrath, but also for conscience sake.
For for this cause ye pay tribute also ; for they are ministers of
God's service, attending continually upon this very thing. Render
to all their dues : tribute to whom tribute is due ; custom to whom
custom ; fear to whom fear ; honour to whom honour."[1] We make
the following observations :

(a) It seems not unlikely that Paul is here echoing the words of
Jesus which we have just been discussing, and the passage must be
read in the light of those words. For Paul is always to be interpreted
by reference to Jesus, not Jesus by reference to Paul. It may be
willingly conceded that Paul, who had himself experienced the
benefits of Roman civil protection and seems to have been more
than a little susceptible to the glamour of the imperial idea,[2] puts
a much greater stress than did Jesus on the duty of civil obedience.
When we remember how he invoked the protection of Roman law,
used the great military roads, relied for security and ease of travel
upon the Pax Romana, it is little wonder that he saw in Roman law
and order a divinely ordained instrument to assist the cause of his
Master. Paul realized, too, the need for effecting a working understanding between Christianity and the civil authority,[3] and saw that
this implied on the part of Christians a willingness to make certain
concessions to the powers that be : they are to be loyal so far as such
loyalty does not violate the higher loyalty due to Christ. It is
interesting, however, to speculate whether Paul would have written
in quite the same terms of the Roman "powers" if this letter had

[1]Rom. xiii. 1–7. Cf. also 1 Pet. ii, 13–14.

[2]He boasts of his Roman citizenship (Acts xxii. 28) ; he saw in Rome's discipline the
force which prevented the final breaking in of the power of anti-Christ (2 Thess.
ii. 7) ; he turns Rome's political system into spiritual metaphors (Phil. iii. 20) ; the
goal of his missionary efforts is the Imperial City herself (Acts xix. 21 ; xxiii. 11).

[3]Similarly this appears to have been one of the motives of the author of the Book
of Acts.

been penned at the close of his own life, still more if he had already seen the beginnings of a general persecution of the Church. The Book of Revelation itself shows the revulsion of feeling of which the Christian Church was capable.

(*b*) When we base an argument on such words as "there is no power but of God ; and the powers that be are ordained of God",[1] it is important to be quite clear, first about Paul's meaning, and second about what we are trying to prove on the basis of that meaning. Does Paul mean that the principle of ordered government for the protection of justice is divinely ordained ? Or does he mean that any particular government, which happens to be in power, is so because God Himself has ordained it ? Clearly the former is the basic truth underlying his words. Yet it is perfectly obvious that the Apostle, believing as he does that on the whole the Roman government is a power for good, writes the words with the particular government of the day in view.[2] But when basing an argument upon Paul's words it is necessary for us to distinguish between the State as such, that is to say the body of citizens in their corporate capacity as the guardian of law and liberty, and the particular Government which happens to be in control at any given time. Some form of "State" we may well admit to be "ordained of God". But to insist upon a perfectly literal acceptance of the surface-meaning of Paul's words is to prove far too much. Not only would the existence of an ordered and authoritative civil government be proved to be "ordained of God", but any gang which might set itself up as "the higher powers", and presumably any policy however godless, would likewise be declared to be "of God". Taking into consideration the circumstances under which Paul writes, and his desire that the infant Church should so far as possible keep on good terms with the civil authority, it is clear that these words of the Apostle must be used with no less careful discrimination than his much less tactful sayings about women and marriage. Yet traditional theology has again and again used the words to support the State's claim to unconditional authority over the will of its subjects.

(*c*) The use commonly made of the words "he beareth not the sword in vain"[3] likewise results in proving far too much. The Apostle, it is argued, is here asserting that "the power" has an absolute and presumptive right to use what force he thinks fit (amounting if necessary to war) for the resistance of evil and the furtherance of State interests. But Paul was writing to the Christians

[1] Rom. xiii. 1.
[2] We feel the same difficulty with reference to the words which the Fourth Evangelist puts on Jesus' lips before Pilate : "Thou wouldest have no power against me, except it were given thee from above."—John xix. 11.
[3] Rom. xiii. 4.

at Rome, to subjects of an empire whose "higher powers" had no thought of limiting the use of force to what would now be considered moral ends. Our opponents cannot have it both ways. They may not claim the support of this text for an anti-pacifist position, and then go on to explain that of course Paul, no less than they themselves, was thinking of the kind of force which a modern "Christian" government would employ. If the words sanction the use of force at all, then it is the kind of force with which Paul's readers were familiar, a use of force which included wars of aggression, the enslavement of captives, the martyring of Christians. Which again suggests that it is well to temper our interpretation of Paul by reference both to Jesus' own teaching and also to the peculiar circumstances under which the Apostle was writing.

(*d*) In any case there is no explicit reference here to war : it is very doubtful whether it is even implicit ; probably the question of war never entered Paul's mind as he wrote these verses. The issue before him is the attitude of the "power" to the good and the bad citizen. Clearly then the "power", as even the wording of the Westminster Confession implies, is the "civil magistrate", and the "sword" is the symbol of the "civil authority". No more may be deduced from the passage than the right of the civil authority to maintain order with a police force, which will restrain the evil-doer and bring him before a responsible judge. The ethical distinction between such measures and the indiscriminate and irresponsible violence used in war, whereby the sword becomes an "avenger for wrath" not only to "him that doeth evil" but to the helpless and innocent, is basic to any sane pacifist position. If it be objected that what is to-day the duty of a police-force was in the Roman world a military function, the reply is that the converse holds good also : it would be just as true to say that, so far as Paul himself had experience of it, the function of the military in the Roman world was the maintenance of civil order. It was thus that Paul knew the Roman soldier, and would doubtless approve of him.

(*e*) The whole passage must then be read as Paul's apology, written under the special circumstances which we have tried to indicate, for a system of civil government, which he admits indeed to be of divine appointment, but would hardly allow to lie within the order of grace as revealed by Christ. Such a Christian order of society rests upon a different and higher principle, which is concisely stated in the very next paragraph[1] ; this may be summarized in its concluding words : "Love worketh no ill to his neighbour : love therefore is the fulfilment of the law." It is only in the light

[1]Rom. xiii. 8-10.

of what follows that we can see these verses, which we have just been discussing, in their true perspective.

(f) It is very important also to recognize the close connection of this section with the great pacifist paragraph, ending with the watchword, "Be not overcome of evil, but overcome evil with good," by which it is immediately preceded.[1] Some of the older commentaries note this connection and explain it thus : the preceding "pacifist" verses have suggested to Paul that he should next go on to safeguard the Christian Ethic, as intended by him to apply in the sphere of individual conduct, against possible misapplication in the sphere of civil obligation. "The idea of the civil power may have been suggested by verse 19 of the preceding chapter, 'Avenge not yourselves', etc., as being one of the ministers of the Divine wrath and retribution ; . . . at any rate the juxtaposition of the two passages would serve to remind St. Paul's readers that the condemnation of individual vengeance and retaliation does not apply to the action of the State in enforcing law ; for the State is God's minister, and it is the just wrath of God which is acting through it."[2]

But it is hardly in the manner of the Apostle, first to expound the very essence of the ethic of Jesus, as he does in xii. 9–21, and then to proceed to qualify it. It is therefore not surprising that our most modern English Commentary on *Romans* treats the present passage not as a qualification of the way of life laid down in the previous chapter, but as an illustration of its application. Thus Professor C. H. Dodd,[3] after quoting the words, "Be not overcome of evil, but overcome evil with good," as "the most creative element in Christian ethics", goes on to show how in the present passage Paul picks out the relation of the Christian to the State as one of the spheres within which he may practise that ethic. The famous words in Romans xiii. are in fact intended to urge upon the Church that same pacifist attitude to the State which was adopted by Jesus Himself. Incipient hostility on the part of the State is to be met not with resistance but with the submissiveness of those who know that "to them that love God all things work together for good".[4] "We can hardly doubt that the possibility existed that the Church might be committed by Jewish-Christian enthusiasts to a disastrous policy of opposition to the Government." The verses in question are therefore "to be read, in the first instance, as a definite repudiation, on behalf of the Church, of the Zealot tendency in Judaism, which was already gathering strength for the final outbreak, and might well have repercussions among Christians. Paul makes his statement

[1]Rom. xii. 17–21.
[2]Sanday and Headlam, *Romans*, in I.C.C., p. 366.
[3]See *Romans*, in the *Moffat New Testament Commentary*, pp. 202–4.
[4]Rom. viii. 28.

quite absolute. Yet he was clearly prepared to disobey in the case of a conflict of loyalties. But he is thinking of contumacious defiance of the Empire such as was advocated by Jewish fanatics. Upon those who rebel, the legal penalty of rebellion will fall ; and this, he seems to imply, is in fact the Divine judgment on their action. It is tempting to see here a reference to the saying attributed to Jesus in Matthew xxvi. 52 : 'Put up again thy sword into its place ; for all they that take the sword shall perish by the sword'." We see, therefore, that these verses, which have too often been used to buttress the State's alleged divinely ordained authority to demand the citizen's service in war, might be much more aptly used to prove that Jesus' pacifist outlook was shared to the full by His great Apostle.

(g) It is now possible to see how the passage fits in with what was said above[1] concerning the "Wrath" of God. The traditional translation of verse 4, "he is a minister of God, an avenger for wrath to him that doeth evil", is somewhat misleading. The magistrate is rather "a divine agent bringing the penalty of Wrath upon the evil-doer". "We then get Paul's theory of civil government in its true setting. It is part of the natural moral order, or divine appointment, but lying outside the order of grace revealed in Christ. It exhibits the principle of retribution just as it is exhibited in the natural laws of cause and effect to which the body and mind of man are subject. . . . The retributive system of justice in a non-Christian society is also a manifestation of the same principle. . . . The Christian takes no part in the administration of a retributive system ; but, in so far as it serves moral ends, he must submit to it."[2]

A study of the earliest Christian interpreters of Scripture shows without any ambiguity the relative value which they placed upon the claims of Caesar and the claims of God. They all echo the Apostles' cry, "We must obey God rather than men."[3] Admittedly, after the end of the second century the evidence of the Christian Fathers is much less unambiguous. The problem is further complicated by the fact that service in the army would involve, not only the violation of a pacifist ethic, but also an oath of loyalty to the Emperor and participation in heathen religious rites. The latter, rather than any objection to war as such, is commonly stated by non-pacifist apologists to be the chief reason for the refusal of Christians to take part in war. The question is much too involved to be treated fully here.[4] But the following two statements may be made with some assurance :

[1] Pp. 56 f.   [2] Dodd, *Romans*, p. 204.   [3] Acts v. 29.
[4] See C. J. Cadoux, *The Early Church and the World*, for an adequate discussion.

Firstly, until about the close of the third quarter of the second century the attitude of the Church was quite consistently pacifist. Harnack's conclusion is that no Christian would become a soldier after Baptism at least up to the time of Marcus Aurelius, say about A.D. 170.[1] After that time signs of compromise become increasingly evident, but the pacifist witness continues strong right up into the fourth century. Aristeides, Justin Martyr, Tatian in the second century, Tertullian, Origen, Cyprian, Hippolytus in the third, Lactantius in the fourth, all make statements which show that they regard war as organized sin and a denial of the way of Jesus. In the Canons of Hippolytus it is stated that a soldier who confesses himself a Christian convert is to be excluded from the sacrament until he has done penance for the blood which he has shed.

Secondly, whatever influence the fear of pagan contamination may have had, when these writers give their reason for denouncing military service, it is nearly always the straight Christian-Pacifist objection which is stated ; war is the antithesis of Christianity: "The weapons of blood are discarded, that the weapons of peace may be girded on." As Harnack again admits, and there is no greater authority on the age in question, the chief reason for the offence which the military profession gave to the earliest Christians was that "it was a war-calling, and Christianity had absolutely renounced war and the shedding of blood". Here are some characteristic statements ; note how again and again the antithesis between Christian discipleship and the soldier's calling is underlined :

Justin Martyr (c. 150) declares that, while Christians will gladly die for Christ's sake, "We refrain from making war on our enemies. . . . For Caesar's soldiers possess nothing which they can lose more precious than their life, while our love goes out to that eternal life which God will give us by His might."[2] Clement of Alexandria, though elsewhere he shows traces of ambiguity, says (c. 200) that Christ "with His word and with His blood gathers the army that sheds no blood". "We Christians", writes Origen (first half of third century) "no longer take up sword against nation, nor do we learn to make war any more, having become children of peace, for the sake of Jesus who is our leader." "As we by our prayers vanquish all demons who stir up war . . . we in this way are much more helpful to the kings than those who go into the field for them. . . . And none fight better for the king than we do. We do not indeed fight under him, although he require it, but we fight on his behalf, forming a special army, an army of piety, by offering our prayers to God."[3] "Shall it be held lawful", asks Tertullian (c. 200), "to

---

[1]Harnack, *Militia Christi*, p. 47 f.   [3]*Contra Celsum*, v. 33 ; viii. 73.
[2]*Apology*, I, II, 39.

make an occupation of the sword, when the Lord proclaims that he who uses the sword shall perish by the sword ? And shall the son of peace take part in battle when it does not become him even to sue at law ?"[1] "How shall a Christian man wage war, nay, how shall he even be a soldier in peace-time, without the sword, which the Lord had taken away ? For although soldiers had come to John, and had received the formula of their rule ; although even a centurion had believed ; the Lord afterwards, in disarming Peter, ungirded every soldier."[2] Cyprian (died 258) protests against the dual standard of morality which brings it about that "if a murder is committed privately it is a crime, but if it happens with State authority courage is the name for it".[3] And as late as the beginning of the fourth century we find Lactantius declaring : "It will not be lawful for a just man to serve as a soldier, for justice itself is his military service, nor to accuse anyone of a capital offence, because it makes no difference whether thou kill with a sword or with a word, since killing itself is forbidden. And so, in this commandment of God, no exception at all ought to be made to the rule that it is always wrong to kill a man, whom God had wished to be regarded as a sacrosanct creature."[4] These statements will appear all the more striking if we remember that they are made by men for whom the Old Testament, with its frequent glorification of nationalism and militarism, was the Word of God in as full a sense as the New. "They were saved", writes Cadoux, "by the soundness of their own moral intuitions from drawing from these ancient precedents the erroneous conclusions affecting their own conduct, which some modern controversialists are so eager to draw from them."[5]

It is suprising that orthodox theology is still so blind to the witness of primitive Christianity, and remains tied hand and foot by the traditional dogma of Church and State which was laboriously evolved from the beginning of the fourth century onwards. For the crucial change in the attitude of the Church to the claims of Caesar began, of course, after the conversion of the Emperor Constantine to Christianity in 312. The Faith was now exalted, or debased, into a State religion, and Christians naturally began to look to the State for patronage, and in return more and more became reconciled to Caesar's claims, even where these might seem to compromise the New Testament ethic. And, as usual, war provides the touch-stone. The result of this changing attitude is thus summarized by Harnack: "After the winning over of Constantine the barrier between the *milites Christi* and the army was removed. The *milites Christi* put

[1] *De Corona*, xi.　　　　[2] *De Idololatria*, xix.　　　　[3] *Epistles*, I, 6.
[4] *Divinae Institutiones*, vi. 20, 15–17.
[5] Cadoux, *The Early Church and the World*, p. 118 ; quoted by Heering, op. cit. p. 47, to whom I also owe several of these quotations.

themselves at the disposal of the Emperor. The soldier of Christ became *ipso facto* a soldier of Caesar."[1] The Church even went the length of pronouncing the primitive Christian attitude liable to punishment, and as early as 314 the Council of Arles decreed that "they who threw away their weapons in time of peace shall be excommunicated". Harnack rightly terms this decision "astonishing and shocking", and adds that by it "the Church completely revised her attitude to the army and war ; . . . She even created saints on behalf of the Christian soldiers, and relegated to the monastic orders her old views about war".[2]

It was Athanasius, "the Father of orthodoxy", who was one of the first to set the seal of official approval upon a subservience to State claims which involves in fact a double-morality ; and once again it is the question of war which provides the test : "Murder is not permitted", he writes, "but to kill one's adversary in war is both lawful and praiseworthy."[3] Augustine, too, vigorously defends the right of the State to require the services of Christians in war, which for him always appears as a police measure against evil-doers. One can almost hear the modern dictator's apology for a "civilizing" war of aggression : "He who is bereft of his freedom, because he misused it by doing evil, is conquered in his own best interests."[4] Yet Augustine is quite obviously troubled in conscience by the dual ethic which his hypothesis involves ; and in his great work *De Civitate Dei* he is the first systematically to define the relations between the Church and the State. He insists that the *Civitas Terrena*, as represented by the Roman Empire, is both ordained of God and under God's sovereignty, and that God righteously uses it as an instrument of war for the accomplishment of His will : "So likewise does He with the times and ends of war, be it His pleasure justly to correct or mercifully to pity mankind, ending them sooner or later, as He wills."[5] Yet he cannot wholly break with the older antithesis between Church and State, for according to him it is only in the *Civitas Dei*, which he practically identifies with the Church, that God's reign is perfectly manifested and the Christian ethic can come to its full expression.

Obviously such a hesitant attempt to harmonize conflicting loyalties could not permanently satisfy the demands of a Catholic theology which was becoming more and more subservient to the State. The dualism between Church and State, so apparent in Augustine's *Civitas Terrena* and *Civitas Dei*, is resolved into a systematic unity by Thomas Aquinas (thirteenth century), who

[1] *Militia Christi*, p. 87.
[2] Op. cit. p. 92.
[3] Athanasius : *Epistle to Ammonius*.
[4] *Epistle to Marcellinus*, xiv.
[5] *De Civ. Dei*, v. 22.

insists far more strongly than Augustine, not only that the political State exists in the providence of God, but also that it is the natural and indispensable foundation of the Kingdom of Grace as represented by the Church. State and Church together thus become a single *corpus Christianum*. The Church might have "conquered" the world, but in at least an equal measure the world had penetrated the Church, and the purity of the Christian ethic suffered correspondingly. Aquinas is still the Catholic apologist *par excellence* for the "just war", when it is "waged by the command of the ruler for a righteous cause and with a good intention." But Catholicism after Aquinas was driven to recognize that the keenest Christian consciences were certain still to feel the tension between the earthly citizenship and the citizenship of the Kingdom of God. It therefore more and more encouraged such to withdraw from the world into the cloister, where alone pure Christian truth might be lived out. Of course this is, in fact, a recognition of a dual Christian standard : and it is still the Roman Catholic solution of the insoluble question, how to preserve both a Christianity which is subservient to a non-Christian or semi-Christian State and also the full Gospel ethic.

The development of Reformed thought is even more significant. Luther, in his revolt against the cloister, was obliged to insist that the pure ethic of the Sermon on the Mount was the true life for every Christian. When compelled to come to some understanding with the State, he still retained the idea of a single *corpus Christianum* ; but he took refuge in the explanation that this "body" consisted of two "domains", a spiritual and a worldly ; the one, in which the Christian is under the sanctifying grace of God, the other "put under the sword", in which by the ordinance of God evil men are kept in restraint and outward peace and order preserved by the State. These two domains demand a different morality ; for the "order of grace" there is a personal morality based on the Sermon on the Mount ; for the "order of creation" there is a State morality ; and only the former is wholly Christian. When we ask, as we are bound to ask, how the Christian who has to live in both these domains can contrive thus to practise a dual morality, Luther replies that in his personal life and relations he must abide by the first order and the full ethic of the Gospel : as a Christian citizen he must abide in loyalty to the second order which is "put under the sword". "In spirit Christians are subject to none but Christ alone, but with life and goods they are nevertheless subject to the secular authority, and obliged to be obedient to it."[1] The antithesis accordingly is now not between two distinct classes of people, as in

[1] *Ob Kriegsleute auch in seligem Stande sein können*, Luthers Werke ; Weimar Ed., XIX, p. 629.

the Catholic solution ; the two conflicting types of ethic are, as Troeltsch puts it, "brought together into a dual way of life for every individual ; the compromise is shifted to more deeply inward ground".[1] Luther frankly draws the conclusion that, whatever be true of the inward personal life, the entire outward life of the Christian is to be in submission to the sovereign and to the sovereign's conception of the will of God. And once again the implications of such a doctrine come out most clearly with respect to war : "The hand which bears such a sword (the sword of government) is as such no longer man's hand but God's ; and not man it is, but God, who hangs, breaks on the wheel, beheads, strangles and wages war. . . . It is not I that smites, thrusts and kills, but God and my Prince, whose servants are my hand and life."[2] When Luther's teaching is thus set forth, it is difficult perhaps to realize that this doctrine is still the orthodox basis in the Protestant world for the dominant view concerning the ethics of Church and State. Yet it can hardly be called a solution of the problem at all ; for man is one personality, and possesses one inward and spiritual life, which, so far from being exclusive of his outward life, is deeply affected by it, and in turn very largely determines it. As Troeltsch justly remarks : "The Protestant way out of the strain of a dual morality, personal and official, is not a solution, but a reformulation of the problem."[3]

It must be confessed that Calvin comes no nearer than does Luther to an adequate solution. While taking over many of Luther's arguments he thinks to avoid the dualistic character of Lutheran ethics, and the discrepancy between personal and State morality, by insisting that God's Word comes to a man in Scripture as a whole, that this Word when related to human conduct comes primarily as a commandment, and that therefore even in the Old Testament commandments, one and all, we are to recognize, not a relatively Christian ethic, but one that is wholly Christian. The obvious contradiction between the thorough-going love-ethic of the Sermon on the Mount and the savage demands of Old Testament nationalism is resolved as follows : God's love is primarily the love of the Sovereign, who by His omnipotence elects some and reprobates others ; similarly man's love is above all else the will to give God the glory that is His due by keeping His commandments, as they are laid down in Old Testament and New Testament alike. Calvin can thus see the *corpus Christianum* as a single, undivided "domain". "God's glory is involved in this alliance of Church and State. And everything that can minister to that glory is not only

[1] *Die Soziallehren der Christlichen Kirchen und Gruppen*, p. 505 ; quoted by Heering, op. cit. p. 75.
[2] *Ob Kriegsleute*, p. 626.   [3] Op. cit. p. 509.

permitted but required, and does not need the expedient of a so-called 'official morality' to justify it."[1] In particular Calvin has no difficulty in justifying war ; for he can always appeal to the Old Testament, with which the Sermon on the Mount, in view of the unity of Scripture, cannot be in conflict. As Heering remarks at the close of an interesting study, "Calvinism has thus solved the problem of Christianity and State morality by bringing the State and its instruments of power under a 'Christian' law, basing this law mainly on the Old Testament, and putting the New Testament motive of love in the background".[2] When it is objected that the New Testament nowhere gives its sanction to war, but rather condemns it outright, Calvin replies that war is a concern of the State, that the causes which the Old Testament heroes found for waging war still remain, and that "in this respect Christ altered nothing whatever by His coming".

It is as well that we should frankly recognize that it is upon this foundation of bad theology and worse Scriptural interpretation that the teaching of the Westminster Confession is based, when it declares in Chapter XXIII, "God, the supreme Lord and King of all the world, hath ordained civil magistrates to be under Him over the people for His own glory and the public good ; and, to this end, hath armed them with the power of the sword, for the defence and encouragement of them that are good, and for the punishment of evil-doers. . . . *Christians . . . may lawfully, now under the New Testament, wage war upon just and necessary occasions.*"[3] If war be, as we believe we have demonstrated, contrary to the ethic of the Gospel, than so long as the Christian citizen assents to the State's claim to wage a "just and necessary" war, just so long is he also assenting to the doctrine of a dual-ethic and a radical distinction between personal and collective morality. The Church has largely lost the moral leadership of the world because it has taken this road of compromise, and to-day even in Christian circles this countenancing, often no doubt almost unconsciously, of such a double standard of morality is playing havoc with the sincerity of our entire Christianity. What is to be the final outcome ? "If Christianity does not set itself against this exalting of the State above morality, the spirit of the world will soon enough break loose from its fastness of non-moral political power, and will gradually re-conquer every region which the Christian conscience has subdued to itself in the course of twenty centuries."[4]

[1]Heering, op. cit. p. 82.   [3]Cf. also the 37th Article of the Church of England.
[2]Op. cit. p. 82.
[4]Max Huber, *Internationale politiek en Evangelie*, p. 26 ; quoted by Heering, op. cit. p. 166.

It is certain that the tension between the ethics of Church and State, between Christ and Caesar, can never wholly be resolved. For both occupy a common field of action on which neither can afford to give way. The Church, no less than the State, is committed to the belief that the life of man finds its meaning and fulfilment only in a community of persons, free persons, but still units in a community. And only in relation to such a community can the Church fulfil her mission. "It is no longer sufficient that the Church should bear its witness only or chiefly to individuals. Its witness can be effective only as a continual challenge and criticism of the prevailing ideas and ways of life, in so far as these are contradictory of the Christian understanding of man and his responsibilities. In a community consciously committed to a contrary view, and most of all where the State has adopted a totalitarian policy, this witness can be borne only at the cost of suffering and martyrdom."[1] Our problem inevitably resolves itself into the question as to where our final loyalty lies ; and the conflict of loyalties can be resolved only in the old way : "We must obey God rather than men."[2] The Christian Pacifist does not deny that the State is a Divine institution ; he only affirms that there are certain State activities which the Christian conscience can never endorse. He gives loyalty due to Caesar, but he also recognizes that a point is sometimes reached when a choice must be made between defiance of Caesar and apostasy from Christ. He is willing to render to Caesar the things that are Caesar's, but only when he is not thereby precluded from rendering to God the things that are God's.

[1] J. H. Oldham, *Church, Community and State*, p. 19.
[2] Acts v. 29.

CHAPTER EIGHT

THE CHALLENGE TO THE CHURCH

THE tension of which we have been speaking has been raised to breaking-point by the Second World War and more recent developments. Area bombing, extermination bombing, the atomic bomb, the napalm bomb in Korea, the threat of germ warfare—all these "improved" methods of warfare have in the sacred name of "military necessity" put the Christian conscience under a compulsion that can no longer be endured. Doubtless the argument that modern war is less defensible ethically than war in the past may be rejected as purely sentimental. The horrors of war can be abolished only when we abolish war itself. Yet one must admit the cogency of the truth, expressed by Hegel in his *Logik*, that all things have their measure and that, when the measure is passed through quantitative alteration, there is a qualitative change also : "things cease to be what they were." There is surely some moral obtuseness about the man who can see no ethical difference between, let us say, the defence of Thermopylae by Leonidas and his Spartans, and the dropping of atomic bombs upon the defence-less population of Hiroshima and Nagasaki.

The cruel dilemma in which the Church was caught, between the Christian necessity of "drawing the line" somewhere and the practical impossibility, under the plea of military necessity, of so doing, became more and more apparent during the course of the late war. "The whole Christian tradition," wrote Dr. J. H. Oldham in the *Christian News Letter* in September, 1940, "is opposed to the view that everything is permissible in war in order to win. . . . I agree that the line is hard to draw : I am sure there is a line to be drawn somewhere. Christianity has no meaning unless for every man there is a point where he says, 'Here I stand before an absolute ; this is unconditionally forbidden'." A month later he was even more emphatic : "The deliberate killing of non-combatants is murder. If war degenerates into wilful slaughter of the innocent, Christians must either become pacifists or give up their religion." But as the war dragged on the line to be drawn was pushed farther and farther back. In May, 1943, we find Dr. Oldham writing : "Where the line is to be drawn between attacks on military targets, on the one hand, and indiscriminate slaughter and wanton destruction, on the other, is a decision which, so far as I can see, must be left to the Government, the military authorities, and the fighting men." And finally two months later : "It is the acceptance of war that increasingly seems to me to be the fundamental issue, while the precise point where the line is to be drawn is of secondary importance. . . . If you accept war, military necessity, in so far as it is a real necessity, must prevail." A tragic landslide surely from Christian standards, and this on the part of a publication which was unrivalled in its efforts to preserve Christian values in the midst of war ! But at least we know where we stand. Once reject uncompromising Christian Pacifism, and the Church is committed (with the assent of its leaders !) to the acceptance of total war, with no moral reservations whatever save such as "military necessity" may allow.

That the pressure upon the Christian conscience had become intolerable was proved at the meeting of the World Council of Churches at Amsterdam in 1948 when a group of non-pacifists, led by the Bishop of Chichester, took up a new position mid-way between pacifist and non-pacifist. The Report of the Council starts with the assertion (which has been reaffirmed at every such conference for the past twenty years) : "We are one in proclaiming to all mankind that war is contrary to the will of God ; war as a method of settling disputes is incompatible with the teaching and example of our Lord Jesus Christ." But there unanimity ends, and the Report goes on to state that "three broad positions are maintained : (1) In the absence of impartial supranational institutions, there are those who hold that military action is the ultimate sanction of the rule of law, and that citizens must be distinctly taught that it is their duty to defend the law by force if necessary. (2) Others, again, refuse military service of all kinds, convinced that an absolute witness against war and for peace is for them the will of God, and they desire that the Church should speak to the same effect. (3) There are those who hold that, even though entering a war may be a Christian's duty in particular circumstances, modern warfare, with its mass destruction, *can never be an act of justice*" (italics mine). It is this third group which represents a new point of view on the part of non-pacifist Christians ; for, though they still defend participation in an activity which they have confessed to be contrary to the will of God, they nevertheless acknowledge that the ostensible aim of any justifiable war, namely the vindication of justice, is in fact unrealizable. "The immense use of air forces and the discovery of atomic and other new weapons render widespread and indiscriminate destruction inherent in the whole conduct of modern war in a sense never experienced in past conflicts. In these circumstances the tradition of a iust war, requiring a just cause and the use of just means, is now challenged. Law may require the sanction of force, but when war breaks out force is used on a scale which tends to destroy the basis on which law exists."

The emergence of this third group in the non-pacifist camp is extraordinarily significant, for it is in fact a confession that the whole theological basis of the Christian non-pacifist position has collapsed. For Catholic and Protestant theologians alike, for Luther and Calvin no less than for Ambrose, Augustine and Thomas Aquinas, the sole apology for waging war has been the traditional doctrine of the "just war." It is on this that rests the statement in the XXXIX Articles that "it is lawful for Christians, at the commandment of the Magistrate, to wear weapons, and serve in the wars" (the wording in the XLII Articles of 1553 is "serve in *lawful* wars"), and in the Westminster Confession of Faith that Christians "may lawfully now under the New Testament wage war upon just and necessary occasions." But all through the centuries theologians have laid down the strictest conditions to which such a "just" war must conform. Indeed the very purpose of the "doctrine" as formulated by successive theologians was (*a*) to provide justification for Christian participation in war, which might otherwise be challenged as contrary to Christian teaching and principle, and (*b*) to lay down conditions defining not only the "just cause" but also, be it noted, the "just means" by which alone such a cause might be legitimately defended. To justify participation by Christians not only must the cause be wholly just, but the means must be "restrained within the limits of justice and love" ; and here the greatest emphasis has always been laid upon the necessity of discrimination between combatants and non-combatants.

Now in theory at least we may still claim that it is possible to determine whether or no a cause is "just". But in practice, once national passions are aroused and mass propaganda is in full swing, can we be confident that it will ever be possible to reach a clear judgment as to even the relative justice of any cause ? It is however with regard to the means of warfare that non-pacifist theologians now find themselves in an *impasse*. In a most significant Report presented by a Special Commission to the General Assembly of the Church of Scotland in 1951 the majority, while still adhering to the traditional non-pacifist position, yet make the following damaging admissions : "Certain features of the war, foreshadowed in the First World War—obliteration bombing, unconditional surrender, mass propaganda, the atomic bomb—raised acute doubts in the minds of many, by no means only of pacifists, as to the relevance of speaking in terms of 'justice' with regard to either the ends or means of modern war." "Our experience of the methods of modern warfare,

G

and our just apprehensions of their future potential extension, have made obsolete most of the traditional distinctions as to 'just means' of warfare." "There is to-day a widespread and well-grounded fear that the results of a major conflict would be conditions of such devastation and anarchy as would destroy the foundations on which justice is possible. This is vividly represented to many minds to-day by the appalling devastation inflicted on the Koreans in the course of a war believed to be justly undertaken against aggression." "We have therefore to acknowledge that any doctrine of the Just War which is based upon the idea of an accepted code of behaviour to be enforced upon, or accepted by, warring powers is unreal in the present circumstances." "We must therefore declare that the methods of modern war are so different from those in the minds of the formulators of the traditional Doctrine as to render many of their arguments irrelevant." Nevertheless, against the logic of their whole argument, the Commission amazingly concludes that "the traditional doctrine of the Just War is still relevant in the conditions of our atomic age", and that there is "no reason to depart from the received teaching that Christians may lawfully wage war upon just and necessary occasions." In the light of its own admissions the Commission surely acknowledges the bankruptcy of non-pacifist theology when it finally confesses that, short of the pacifist position, "we can see no Christian alternative to the statement of the Westminster Confession."

To claim that war even for a just cause can itself be a "just war" irrespective of the means employed is possible only on the assumption that the end justifies the means, however unjust the latter may in itself be. But to admit that necessity knows no law and that a worthy end justifies the means however sinful, is surely the final betrayal of Christian principle. "Nothing is more terrible", writes Jacques Maritain, "more cause of scandal, than to see . . . evil barbarous means employed by men claiming to act in the name of Christian order. . . . The character of the end is already predetermined in the means. . . . It is a truth inscribed in the very nature of things, that Christendom will recreate itself by Christian means, or it will perish completely." In view of the virtual collapse of the doctrine of the "Just War" non-pacifists are left without any theological standing-ground. If the non-pacifist majority in the Church are to maintain their position, then it appears that they must restate their case on a basis quite different from that adopted by the majority at Amsterdam, namely that "military action is the ultimate sanction of the rule of law." Of such a restatement there is up to date no sign whatever : failing it, Pacifists may well claim that their case wins by default.

Why is it then that the vast majority of thoughtful Christians, most of them just as sincere in their convictions as are Christian Pacifists, still fail to find in the New Testament a clear condemnation, in all conceivable circumstances, of participation in war ? We have already considered in Chapters Three and Four some of the arguments which have been used to "water down" what to a Pacifist appears to be self-evident truth. But to-day it is the orthodox Protestant theologians, particularly the dialectical school, who are the chief champions of the non-pacifist position ; and foremost among them is Reinhold Niebuhr, whose writing have perhaps done more than anything else to salve the uncomfortable conscience of the non-pacifist, and even to wean many Pacifists from the pure milk of their faith.[1]

The argument runs somewhat as follows : (1) We must start from the basic fact of human sin. Pacifists are deluded because they reject the Christian doctrine of original sin, and imagine that man is essentially good at some level of his being, and therefore able to respond to the demands of an ethic of absolute love. The truth is that the inherent sinfulness of human nature expresses itself in a "will-to-live" and a "will-to-power" that are diametrically opposed to Jesus' ethic, which finds a man's fullest attainment in a willingness to "lose his life," and insists that the way of greatness is the way of humble service. Even the sincerest Christian is therefore quite incapable of obedience to the way of Christ. Though we know that we ought to love our neighbours as ourselves, there is "a law in our members which wars against the law that is in our mind," so that in fact we love first and foremost our own selves. And if this be true of the Christian individual, much more it is true of social, political and national groups. For it is one of Niebuhr's postulates that "human collectives are less moral than the individuals which compose them." Who looking at the world to-day can deny that the collective sin of man against man has reached diabolical proportions ? And what possible relevance can an ethic of absolute love have in such a world ?

(2) Secondly, given a sinful world and the impracticability of the way of absolute love, the nearest approximation to the ideal is to be found in "equal justice." This, rather than love, is the only practical guide to conduct in the dealings of individual with individual, and still more of community with community ; and because all men are sinners justice can be achieved only by the strict maintenance of

[1]For a fuller treatment of Niebuhr's views see the present writer's *Relevance of the Impossible* (Fellowship of Reconciliation).

law. This in turn demands a certain degree of just coercion on the one hand, and resistance to unjust coercion and tyranny on the other hand; and in the last resort military action is the ultimate sanction of the rule of law.

(3) Thirdly, it follows that the full Christian ethic is not immediately applicable to social and international problems. At most it has a merely relative relevance. It provides us with an ideal standard against which we can measure the magnitude of our past failures, and an ultimate criterion by which every attempt to build a better world must be judged. But also, and for Niebuhr most significantly, the ethic of absolute love gives us "a principle of discriminate criticism between forms of justice." That is to say, when there are two or more alternatives, both admittedly falling short of the ideal, the law of love provides the measuring-stick by which we may determine which of these several "second-bests" approximates most closely to the ideal. It may even lay upon us the duty of accepting what, in the light of the ideal, is not "the best of several second bests" but rather "the less of two *evils*"—for example, according to Niebuhr, war rather than submission to tyranny. The Christian Pacifist is blameworthy because he too often refuses to make such relative judgments, to discriminate between alternative second-bests, to choose the lesser of two evils, and with a good conscience to act upon such a choice.

This is a powerful argument. Has the New Testament any answer ? Take first the primacy given to "equal justice" as the goal of Christian action. The plain truth is that the New Testament has surprisingly little to say on the subject ; indeed "justice" can hardly be said to be a New Testament category at all ! And the reason is plain enough. In Chapter Six we tried to show how Jesus taught that the Law, which is the foundation of any "equal justice", finds its only true "fulfilment" in His own new ethic, and in particular in the specifically "pacifist" features in it. That is to say, Jesus did not regard "justice" as an end in itself. He taught that justice truly "fulfilled" is nothing less than love, rather than love a by-product of justice ; that if we aim at love we shall establish justice by the way ; that we can in fact secure Niebuhr's "equal justice" only when we aim primarily not at it, but at the love-relationship of which justice is but an uncompleted part. But in the light of what we have written above concerning the collapse of the traditional doctrine of the Just War, this charge that Pacifism betrays justice through the exaltation of love is little more than academic. It comes ill from those who have at last been compelled themselves to admit that even war in a just cause can now no longer itself be called an "act of justice."

But what of the argument that man is so corrupted by sin as to be incapable, even if he would, of obedience to the ethic of love ? Over against the facile and shallow humanism of yesterday this is no doubt a much-needed corrective. The New Testament has no false optimism about man, and no illusions about the radical nature of sin and evil. Yet from beginning to end it is throbbing with joy and hope, simply because its writers are conscious that a new Power has come into the world to transform it. Jesus Himself can hardly have shared Niebuhr's view of human nature ! When He wished to teach us what God is like He pointed to the God-like in men. Even in the worst sinner He could discover the hidden good and appeal to it, knowing that the good and not the evil is the essential man. He tells us that it is when a sinner "comes to himself" that he "arises and goes to his Father" : the man's true self is that within him which responds to God. We may appeal furthermore to the New Testa-ment doctrine of the Holy Spirit and of "enabling grace" which the dialectical theologians so strangely ignore. As Charles Raven has said, "Our discipleship is not our own ; we are not living in our own strength ; we are vitalised and controlled by the good gift of the Holy Ghost. Humanly speaking our task is impossible ; Chris-tianly speaking our resources are infinite."[1] St. Paul at least clearly believed in such "enabling grace." Otherwise how can he speak of "his power that worketh in me mightily," or pray to be "strength-ened with might by His Spirit in the inner man," or boast that "I can do all things through Christ which strengtheneth me" ? Indeed for Paul every step towards the attainment of the Christian ideal is a "fruit of the Spirit," that is a product of the new life of which the Spirit is the author : and this new life is the first result of the Christian's status "in Christ." "If any man be in Christ there is a new creation" : consequently "the servant of Christ is capable of a perfect obedience because he has been transformed in the very constitution of his being".[2] Henceforward the moral demands of the Christian ethic become "the law of the Spirit" and are sponta-neously and joyfully obeyed. Furthermore, if it be argued that the essential immorality of collective man justifies the application of a lower ethical standard to the community than to individuals (an idea which Dean Inge has called "that ruinous dualism of public and private ethics . . . which by openly proclaiming that the teaching of Christ has no reference to the conduct of States has made modern Europe a hell upon earth"[3]) we reply that according to the New Testament it is not in the individual but in the Church as the

[1] *The Theological Basis of Christian Pacifism*, 31.
[2] E. F. Scott, *The Spirit in the New Testament*, 140.
[3] *The Fall of the Idols*, 179.

redeemed community that the work of the Holy Spirit is most powerfully manifested. The existence of such a "fellowship of the Spirit" surely disproves the stark pessimism of *Moral Man and Immoral Society* with its thesis that collective man can never rise above the moral level of a mob, and must always and only act in his own self-interest. Remember that we are speaking of "the Church which is His Body", and that our concern at the moment is not Pacifism as a practical political policy, but the Church's duty and her capacity for obedience.

Finally what of the argument that in the practical affairs of everyday life, and particularly in social and international relation-ships, the full Christian ethic is impossible of achievement, and has therefore merely a relative relevance ? Here too the New Testament doctrine of the Holy Spirit is very much to the point. As William Robinson has splendidly said : "A Christian attitude which neglects the power of the Holy Spirit will regard the Christian ethic as an 'impossible possible', that is, as an *ideal* which can never in any sense be achieved. But an attitude which takes fully into account the power of the Holy Spirit will regard the Christian ethic as a 'possible impossible', that is, as a *reality* beyond mere human achievement, but not beyond the achievement of God through a faithful Church. The Church is not set in the world to achieve a *mundane* 'possible', but to achieve a *heavenly* 'impossible' ; in other words she is set in the world to work 'the works of God'."[1] Indeed one of the most tragic features in the present lamentable world-situation has been the Church's failure to use the power which, in Jesus Christ and His Spirit, God has placed in her hands, and which through the Church's obedience might have been released for the world's redemption. Christian Pacifists have often been warned by self-styled "realists" that we shall never bring in the Kingdom of God by acting in an evil world as if it were already here. Yet this is, I suggest, exactly what Jesus *did* teach : if only men were prepared to take God at His word, and to order their lives here and now by the laws of a transcendent Kingdom, then the power of God would answer the cry of faith, and the Kingdom would break in upon them and take them unawares. After all, if Jesus' ethical teaching is really irrelevant in this present sinful world, so also is His whole work of redemption. For, as William Robinson again writes : "There is no possibility of separating the ethic of Jesus from who Jesus is . . . If we cannot have the ethic apart from the Man, neither can we have the Man apart from the ethic. The ethic expresses the Spirit of Christ and reveals the character of God. If it is not to be practised, and is indeed impracti-

---

[1] *Evil Confronted*, 8 (Fellowship of Reconciliation).

cable, then Christ Himself and His passion and death become equally irrelevant in the kind of world that He lived in and we live in. Both have relevance only for an ideal world other than one of flesh and blood. Christianity then falls under the judgement of being no more than a celestial soporific."[1]

There is no more suble argument against Christian Pacifism than this plea that the ethic of Jesus has merely a relative relevance and that the Christian must therefore be prepared to accept "the lesser of two evils." Let us look at it a little more closely in the light of the New Testament. "The choice," writes John Lewis in his *Case against Pacifism*, "is never between rigid obedience to the moral law and wilful transgression but . . . between two courses *both of which have evil consequences.*" Now the words in italics (mine) are dangerously ambiguous. Consequences may be "evil" in the sense that they involve evil-doing and therefore sin ; or they may be "evil" in the sense that they involve material loss or suffering or even death. Now it is likely that any one of us may be confronted with a situation when every possible alternative line of action involves "evil" in the second sense. But "evil" in the first sense ? The New Testament would be reduced to nonsense if we were compelled to believe that God ever places a Christian in an *impasse* to escape from which he is compelled of deliberate choice to commit sin, the "lesser" rather than the greater sin no doubt, but nevertheless sin. "God is faithful . . . who will with the temptation also make a *way of escape.*" Between two ways of sinning there is always a "third alternative" ; it may be a very costly way both for ourselves and for those dear to us ; it may indeed, as it was in Jesus' case, be the way of the Cross. But it is there to be taken, if only the Church has the courage and the faith.

Consider once again Jesus' dilemma as He faced the crisis of His own ministry. Was He caught in this kind of impasse from which there was no escape except by the choice of "the lesser evil" ? He might have argued that the cause for which He stood was so precious that it would be a lesser evil to call up His "twelve legions of angels" and annihilate the evil men who were plotting His destruction, than to see His disciples scattered as the result of His death, and His friends suffering, and His kingdom going down, as must have seemed inevitable, in irretrievable ruin. He might have refused at that point to be bound by the law of absolute love which He Himself had preached. He might have said, "I have the choice of two evils, to see my Gospel destroyed, or to destroy my enemies. I must choose the lesser evil. I must destroy these evil men." But Jesus refused to be caught in this dilemma ; He refused thus to try to calculate

[1] op. cit. 4–5.

consequences ; He believed that sacrificial love was a creative power which could completely change a situation and create the most unexpected consequences. And so He chose the Cross ; and the consequence was not the eclipse of His cause, but its victory ; not only Calvary but also the Resurrection.

What then of this argument that in a national emergency the Christian must be prepared to participate in war as the "lesser evil" ? Pacifists are not alone in questioning the quite unwarrantable assumption that war is in fact always, or ever, the lesser evil. As Dean Inge, not himself a Pacifist, puts it : "The burden of proof always lies with the nation that chooses war, and the reasons alleged are generally, in part at least, hypocritical. That war is the greatest evil in human life, and that no good can ever come of it, are in my opinion certain."[1] But granted that to many the consequences of Pacifism may seem likely to be more evil than war itself, we Christians have no right thus to calculate consequences. We may, like Jesus, seem likely to fail the whole way to Calvary. But the first question is not, What will be the consequences ? or Will the pacifist way "work" ? The first question is, Is it Christ's way ? And if the answer is "yes", then we have no right to calculate the consequences of our choice, because it is just at that point of choice, just by choosing what we know to be the way of Christ, that we open the door for the inrush of God's own power, which, if only we had faith, might so incalculably transform the whole situation as to confound our fears about the consequences of refusing war. And if not ? Why then there is still the way of the Cross, for individuals and for nations alike. And even for a nation the Cross might mean Resurrection and ultimate victory. As Dean Inge again insists, "The notion of a martyr-nation, giving itself up to injustice and spoilation for the most sacred of all causes, cannot be dismissed with contempt."[2]

The Christian Church to-day is challenged to take the lead in a crusade for world peace. The very word "peace" has become so suspect that it seldom appears in print save in inverted commas ! It is for the Church to rehabilitate it ; and no institution in existence has such a comprehensive, world-wide organisation wherewith to take the initiative in so great a task. If our Church leaders suspect, as well they may, the motives of sundry other self-styled champions of "peace", then let the Church herself be in the vanguard of an equally devoted and enthusiastic campaign in the name of the Prince of Peace. Nothing would more surely recreate her own life ; for as the World Council of Churches confessed at Amsterdam, "the Church appears impotent to deal with the realities of the human

[1] *The Fall of the Idols*, 185.
[2] op. cit. 201.

situation because it has failed to speak effectively on the subject of war." If that effective word were spoken, and an effective lead given, it is certain that the people would rally to the Church as they have not done for three or four generations.

As a first step in this new lead the Church will declare her refusal to countenance war under any circumstances whatever, partly because even such a bare act of renunciation will signify a clean cut with the policy which has led to the present tragic "Fall of Christianity," but chiefly because such a refusal is a necessary clearing of the decks for a positive campaign of reconciliation which must otherwise inevitably be stultified from the outset. Moreover she will announce to the world that her refusal to contenance war is absolute. To the objection that the essence of Christian living is not to bind oneself in advance, but to seek to read the will of God in each new situation as it arises, the Church will reply that every new situation grows out of a previous one, and that to fail to break with the errors of the past is to share the guilt of creating a "new situation" in which the way of Christ will be no less "impracticable" than it is declared to be to-day. There can be no question that if all Christians were to announce that henceforth they would refuse absolutely to participate in warfare ; if the Church as such were to give notice that under no conditions would she give her official sanction and spiritual blessing to war measures ; and if this pronouncement were made on the definite basis of unalterable Christian principle, so that governments might know that no amount of pressure or propaganda would move millions of their best citizens to break a vow made before God—then the whole world situation might well be radically changed. The ideal, of course, would be action by the Church Catholic and Universal, or at least by the World Council of Churches. Failing that one national Church must take the initiative. Until it does so, individual Christians must continue to bear unremitting witness. After all, is not that the story of almost all the great redemptive movements of mankind ?

Meanwhile we Christian Pacifists must learn to face the possible cost of peace. The man who in his own soul's life has experienced the miracle of reconciliation finds that a new obligation has been laid upon him. Himself reconciled to God through the sacrificial love of Jesus Christ, he knows himself to be called to serve that same holy love, and to follow that same reconciling way in all his dealings with his fellow-men, and to do so even when the way of obedience seems likely to be the way of appalling risk. It lead Jesus to the Cross. But beyond the Cross was the Resurrection ; and it was Jesus Crucified and Risen who, when "the disciples were assembled in fear, . . . stood in the midst and said unto them, Peace be unto you."

APPENDIX

THE NEW TESTAMENT SPEAKS

THE ROOTS OF WAR

"Whence come wars and whence come fightings among you ? Come they not hence, even of your pleasures that war in your members ? Ye lust, and have not : ye kill, and covet, and cannot obtain : ye fight and war ; ye have not because ye ask not." (James iv. 1 f.)

"The works of the flesh are manifest, which are these . . . enmities, strife, jealousies, wraths, factions, divisions . . . of the which I forewarn you, . . . that they which practise such things shall not inherit the kingdom of God. But the fruit of the Spirit is . . . peace . . . Against such there is no law." (Gal. v. 19–23.)

"Ye cannot serve God and mammon." (Matt. vi. 24.)

THE WAY OF PEACE

"Glory to God in the highest, and on earth peace among men of good-will." (Luke ii. 14.)

"Peace I leave with you ; my peace I give unto you : not as the world giveth give I unto you." (John xiv. 27.)

"Blessed are the peacemakers : for they shall be called sons of God." (Matt. v. 9.)

"The fruit of righteousness is sown in peace for them that make peace." (Jas. iii. 18.)

"How beautiful are the feet of them that preach the gospel of peace." (Rom. x. 15.)

"Stand therefore . . . having shod your feet with the preparation of the gospel of peace." (Eph. vi. 14 f.)

"I therefore, the prisoner in the Lord, beseech you to walk worthily of the calling wherewith ye were called, with all lowliness and meekness, with longsuffering, forbearing one another in love ; giving diligence to keep the unity of the Spirit in the bond of peace." (Eph. iv. 1–3.)

"Follow after peace with all men, and the sanctification without which no man shall seek the Lord." (Heb. xii. 14.)

"The God of peace shall bruise Satan under your feet shortly." (Rom. xvi. 20.)

"Finally, brethren . . . be perfected ; be comforted ; be of the same mind; live in peace : and the God of love and peace shall be with you." (2 Cor. xiii. 11.)

"The peace of God, which passeth all understanding, shall guard your hearts and your thoughts in Christ Jesus." (Phil. iv. 7.)

THE VICTORY OF SELFLESSNESS

"Take my yoke upon you and learn of me ; for I am meek and lowly in heart : and ye shall find rest unto your souls." (Matt. xi. 29.)

"Have this mind in you, which was also in Christ Jesus : who, existing in the form of God, counted not the being on an equality with God a thing to be grasped, but emptied himself, taking the form of a servant. . . . He humbled himself, becoming obedient even unto death, yea, the death of the cross. Wherefore also God highly exalted him, and gave unto him the name which is above every name ; that in the name of Jesus every knee should bow." (Phil. ii. 5–10.)

"Blessed are the poor in spirit: for theirs is the kingdom of heaven. Blessed are the meek : for they shall inherit the earth." (Matt. v. 3, 5.)

"Ye know that the rulers of the Gentiles lord it over them, and their great ones exercise authority over them. Not so shall it be among you : but whosoever would become great among you shall be your minister ; and whosoever would be first among you shall be your servant ; even as the Son of man came not to be ministered unto, but to minister, and to give his life a ransom for many." (Matt. xx. 25–8.)

"Whosoever shall exalt himself shall be humbled ; and whosoever shall humble himself shall be exalted." (Matt. xxiii. 12.)

"God resisteth the proud, but giveth grace to the humble. Humble yourselves therefore under the mighty hand of God, that he may exalt you in due time." (1 Pet. v. 5 f.)

THE COMMANDMENT OF LOVE

"Thou shalt love the Lord thy God with all thy heart, and with all thy soul, and with all thy mind. This is the great and first commandment. And a second like unto it is this, Thou shalt love thy neighbour as thyself. On these two commandments the whole law hangeth." (Matt. xxii. 37–40.)

"The whole law is fulfilled in one word, even in this ; Thou shalt love thy neighbour as thyself." (Gal. v. 14.)

"Love worketh no ill to his neighbour : love therefore is the fulfilment of the law. . . . Owe no man anything, save to love one another." (Rom. xiii. 10, 8.)

"Love your enemies, and pray for them that persecute you ; that ye may be sons of your Father which is in heaven." (Matt. v. 44 f.)

"A new commandment I give unto you, that ye love one another ; even as I have loved you, that ye also love one another. By this shall all men know that ye are my disciples." (John xiii. 34 f.)

"If a man say, I love God, and hateth his brother, he is a liar : for he that loveth not his brother whom he hath seen, cannot love God whom he hath not seen." (1 John iv. 20.)

"Love suffereth long, and is kind ; love . . . seeketh not its own, is not provoked, taketh not account of evil ; . . . beareth all things, believeth all things, hopeth all things, endureth all things. Love never faileth." (1 Cor. xiii. 4 ff.)

"The Lord make you to increase and abound in love toward one another, and toward all men." (1 Thess. iii. 12.)

"Seeing ye have purified your souls in your obedience to the truth unto unfeigned love of the brethren, love one another from the heart fervently." (1 Pet. i. 22.)

"Above all things be fervent in your love among yourselves; for love covereth a multitude of sins." (1 Pet. iv. 8.)

THE DUTY OF FORGIVENESS

"Jesus said, Father forgive them ; for they know not what they do." (Luke xxiii. 34.)

"Whensoever ye stand praying, forgive, if ye have aught against any one ; that your Father also which is in heaven may forgive you your trespasses." (Mark xi. 25.)

"If thy brother sin, rebuke him ; and if he repent, forgive him. And if he sin against thee seven times in the day, and seven times turn again to thee saying, I repent ; thou shalt forgive him." (Luke xvii. 3 f.)

"Put on therefore . . . a heart of compassion . . . forbearing one another, and forgiving each other, if any man have a complaint against any ; even as the Lord forgave you, so also do ye." (Col. iii. 12 f.)

"Let all bitterness, and wrath, and anger, and clamour, and railing, be put away from you, with all malice : and be ye kind one to another, tender-hearted, forgiving each other, even as God also in Christ forgave you." (Eph. iv. 31 f.)

CHRIST'S WAY OF MEETING EVIL

"Christ also suffered for you, leaving you an example, that ye should follow his steps : who did no sin, neither was guile found in his mouth : who, when he was reviled, reviled not again ; when he suffered threatened not ; but committed himself to him that judgeth righteously." (1 Pet. ii. 21 ff.)

"I came not to judge the world, but to save the world." (John xii. 47.)

"When his disciples saw this, they said, Lord, wilt thou that we bid fire to come down from heaven, and consume them ? But he turned and rebuked them." (Luke ix. 54 f.)

"Being reviled, we bless ; being persecuted, we endure ; being defamed, we intreat." (1 Cor. iv. 12.)

"One only is the lawgiver and judge, even he who is able to save and to destroy : but who art thou that judgest thy neighbour ?" (Jas. iv. 12.)

"All things therefore whatsoever ye would that men should do unto you, even so do ye also unto them." (Matt. vii. 12.)

"Love your enemies, do good to them that hate you, bless them that curse you, pray for them that despitefully use you." (Luke vi. 27 f.)

"Resist not him that is evil : but whosoever smiteth thee on thy right cheek, turn to him the other also." (Matt. v. 39.)

"Why not rather take wrong ? Why not rather be defrauded ?" (1 Cor. vi. 7.)

"The Lord's servant must not strive, but be gentle towards all . . . forbearing in meekness, correcting them that oppose themselves." (2 Tim. ii. 24.)

"Bless them that persecute you ; bless, and curse not. . . . Render to no man evil for evil. . . . If it be possible, as much as in you lieth, be at peace with all men. Avenge not yourselves, beloved, but give place unto wrath : for it is written, Vengeance belongeth unto me ; I will recompense, saith the Lord. But if thine enemy hunger, feed him ; if he thirst, give him to drink : for in so doing thou shalt heap coals of fire upon his head. Be not overcome of evil, but overcome evil with good." (Rom. xii. 14 ff.)

"See that none render unto any one evil for evil ; but always follow after that which is good, one toward another, and toward all." (1 Thess. v. 15.)

"Finally, be ye all likeminded, compassionate, loving as brethren, tenderhearted, humbleminded : not rendering evil for evil, or reviling for reviling ; but contrariwise blessing ; for hereunto were ye called, that ye should inherit a blessing." (1 Pet. iii. 8 f.)

THE WAY OF THE CROSS

"God commendeth his own love towards us, in that, while we were yet sinners, Christ died for us." (Rom. v. 8.)

"Jesus the author and perfecter of our faith, who for the joy that was set before him endured the cross, despising shame." (Heb. xii. 2.)

"Forasmuch then as Christ suffered in the flesh, arm ye yourselves also with the same mind." (1 Pet. iv. 1.)

"We are pressed on every side, yet not straitened ; perplexed, yet not unto despair ; pursued, yet not forsaken ; smitten down, yet not destroyed ; always bearing about in the body the dying of Jesus, that the life also of Jesus may be manifested in our body." (2 Cor. iv. 8–10)

"If any man would come after me, let him deny himself and take up his cross and follow me." (Matt. xvi. 24.)

"Wherefore Jesus also, that he might sanctify the people through his own blood, suffered without the gate. Let us therefore go forth unto him without the camp, bearing his reproach." (Heb. xiii. 12 f.)

THE MINISTRY OF RECONCILIATION

"If, while we were enemies, we were reconciled to God through the death of his Son, much more, being reconciled, shall we be saved by his life ; and not only so, but we also rejoice in God through our Lord Jesus Christ, through whom we have now received the reconciliation." (Rom. v. 10 f.)

"It was the good pleasure of the Father that in him should all the fulness dwell ; and through him to reconcile all things unto himself, having made peace through the blood of his cross." (Col. i. 19 f.)

"He is our peace, who made both one, and brake down the middle wall of partition, having abolished in his flesh the enmity . . . that he might create in himself of the twain one new man, so making peace ; and might reconcile them both in one body unto God through the cross, having slain the enmity thereby : and he came and preached peace to you that were far off, and peace to them that were nigh." (Eph. ii. 14–17.)

"All things are of God, who reconciled us to himself through Christ, and gave unto us the ministry of reconciliation ; to wit, that God was in Christ reconciling the world unto himself, not reckoning unto them their trespasses, and having committed unto us the word of reconciliation." (2 Cor. v. 18 f.)

THE FAMILY OF NATIONS

"I bow my knees unto the Father, from whom every family in heaven and on earth is named." (Eph. iii. 14 f.)

"Wherefore, putting away falsehood, speak ye truth each one with his neighbour : for we are members one of another." (Eph. iv. 25.)

"In one spirit were we all baptized into one body, whether Jews or Greeks, whether bond or free ; and were all made to drink of one Spirit." (1 Cor. xii. 13.)

"For there is no distinction between Jew and Greek : for the same Lord is Lord of all, and is rich unto all that call upon him." (Rom. x. 12.)

"There can be neither Jew nor Greek, there can be neither bond nor free, there can be no male or female : for ye are all one man in Christ Jesus." (Gal. iii. 28.)

"There cannot be Greek or Jew, circumcision and uncircumcision, barbarian, Scythian, bondman, freeman ; but Christ is all, and in all." (Col. iii. 11.)

THE MORAL EQUIVALENT OF WAR

"Fight the good fight of faith, lay hold on the life eternal." (1 Tim. vi. 12)

"This is the victory that hath overcome the world, even our faith." (1 John v. 4.)

"For though we walk in the flesh, we do not war according to the flesh (for the weapons of our warfare are not of the flesh, but mighty before God to the casting down of strong holds); casting down imaginations, and every high thing that is exalted against the knowledge of God, and bringing every thought into captivity to the obedience of Christ." (2 Cor. x. 3–5.)

"For our wrestling is not against flesh and blood, but against the principalities, against the powers, against the world-rulers of this darkness, against the spiritual hosts of wickedness in the heavenly places. Wherefore take up the whole armour of God, that ye may be able to withstand in the evil day, and, having done all, to stand." (Eph. vi. 12 f.)

"Take thy part in suffering hardship, as a good soldier of Christ Jesus." (2 Tim. ii. 3.)

"I have fought the good fight, I have finished the course, I have kept the faith : henceforth there is laid up for me the crown of righteousness, which the Lord, the righteous judge, shall give to me at that day : and not only to me, but also to all them that have loved his appearing." (2 Tim. iv. 7 f.)

INDEX OF SCRIPTURE PASSAGES

THE RELEVANCE OF AN IMPOSSIBLE IDEAL

PREFACE TO NEW EDITION

THIS book was first published in 1941 and many of the references and quotations inevitably date it as a war-time production. That the main argument is still felt to be relevant seems indicated by the demand on both sides of the Atlantic for a new edition. I have therefore thought it best to re-issue the book unchanged, apart from the omission of the Appendix to the first edition and the rewriting of the closing paragraphs. I am conscious that some apology is due to Professor Niebuhr for entering the lists again against him without taking into account his more recent writings. But I hope that he will feel that the first chapter is still a fair summary of his challenging argument against Christian pacifism and that the rest of the book is at least a sincere attempt to meet it.

G. H. C. MACGREGOR

The University of Glasgow,
   August, 1959

CHAPTER ONE

NIEBUHR'S CASE STATED

IN the perennial debate concerning the bearing of the New Testament ethic upon the question of peace and war no one has had more influence recently than Reinhold Niebuhr. To the non-pacifist majority in the churches his writings have come as a veritable godsend, and no one has been so successful in salving the conscience of the non-pacifist, and even in weaning the pacifist from the pure milk of his faith. And no wonder! For Niebuhr is an intensely acute and virile thinker, and his argument has a forceful-ness and persuasiveness that set him almost alone among the advocates of Christian non-pacifism. His views concerning pacifism are set forth in his recent booklet *Why the Christian Church is not Pacifist*, which must be read in the light of his three books, *Moral Man and Immoral Society*, *Beyond Tragedy*, and especially *An Interpretation of Christian Ethics*. Niebuhr is not an easy man to read, for unfortunately his trenchancy is not matched by his lucidity. Hence a summary of his argument may be helpful. There is, I believe, a convincing Christian pacifist answer to Niebuhr's position and to offer this is the aim of this booklet. But first we must try thoroughly to understand the formidable case which we have to meet.

Niebuhr's indictment of pacifism may be stated under three heads.

The False Optimism of Christian Pacifism

Firstly, pacifists are misled by the belief that "man is essentially good at some level of his being,"[1] while they have "rejected the Christian doctrine of original sin as an outmoded bit of pessimism."[2] According to Niebuhr "a theology which thus fails to come to grips with the tragic fact of sin is heretical."[3] Like liberal Christianity in general, pacifism has "adopted the simple expedient of denying, in effect, the reality of evil in order to maintain its hope in the triumph of the ideal of love in the world."[4] Hence the baseless optimism which interprets world history "as a gradual ascent to the Kingdom of God, which waits for final triumph only upon the willingness of

---

[1] *Why the Christian Church is Not Pacifist*, 14. [2] Ibid., 12. [3] Ibid., 27.
[4] *An Interpretation of Christian Ethics*, 153.

Christians to take Christ seriously".[1] Hence, too, our naïve faith in "simple" solutions for the world's complex ills, our belief that "if only men loved one another, all the . . . horrible realities of the political order could be dispensed with".[2] Indeed, the issue between pacifist and non-pacifist is "between those who have a confidence in human nature, which human nature cannot support, and those who have looked too deeply into life and their own souls to place their trust in so broken a reed".[3]

The Fallacy of "Non-resistance"

Secondly, this failure to recognize the reality and power of the evil inherent in human nature breeds a child-like confidence in the practicability and efficacy of "non-resistance" as a method of overcoming evil, even in the field of social and political relationships. Such "non-resistance" is, for Niebuhr, the core of the pacifist ethic. Yet, he argues, in believing that non-resistance, or forgiveness, is a means of overcoming evil in an enemy, the pacifist is reading into the New Testament something that is not there: "Nothing is said about the possibility of transmuting enmity to friendship through the practice of forgiveness".[4] The disciple's aim in non-resistance is not to overcome evil in another, but to discipline his own life and make it more worthy of the Kingdom. The pacifist, moreover, half-conscious that non-resistance can have no immediate relevance to any political situation, construes Jesus' summons to non-resistance as if it were one to "non-violent resistance". Yet this again is to read back into Jesus' teaching what is in fact the pacifist's own misinterpretation of it: "There is not the slightest support in Scripture for this doctrine of non-violence. Nothing could be plainer than that the ethic uncompromisingly enjoins non-resistance and not non-violent resistance".[5] Niebuhr would doubtless add that the pacifist has been led astray by a muddled suspicion that, whereas non-violent resistance may possibly "work", absolute non-resistance obviously will not. This confusion of "pragmatic" with purely religious motives and arguments is another charge brought against pacifists. "If Christians are to live by 'the way of the Cross' they ought to practise non-resistance. They will find nothing in the Gospels which justifies non-violent resistance as an instrument of love-perfectionism. . . . The principal defect of the liberal Christian thought on the question of violence is that it confuses two perspectives upon the problem, the pragmatic and the perfectionist one. Both have their own legitimacy. But moral confusion results from

---

[1]*Why the Christian Church is Not Pacifist*, 30.   [2]Ibid., 23.
[3]*An Interpretation of Christian Ethics*, 131.   [4]Ibid., 51.
[5]*Why the Christian Church is not Pacifist*, 17.

efforts to compound them".[1] Such moral confusion is indicated
when pacifists "praise the peace of tyranny as if it were nearer to
the peace of the Kingdom of God than war",[2] for "the introduction
of perfectionist ideas into politics for the purpose of reinforcing
counsels of submission to injustice smells of dishonesty".[3]

The Isolating of a Single Issue

Thirdly, pacifists with their obsession concerning war unjustifiably isolate one particular moral issue, and demand with reference
to it an absolute obedience to Jesus' teaching that they are not
prepared to give over the whole range of life. Here Niebuhr is quite
merciless: "If pacifists were less anxious to dilute the ethic of
Christ to make it conform to their particular type of non-violent
politics, and if they were less obsessed with the obvious contradiction between the ethic of Christ and the fact of war, they might
have noticed that the injunction 'resist not evil' is only part and
parcel of a total ethic which we violate, not only in war-time, but
every day of our life".[4] And again: "The Christian who lives in
and benefits from a society in which coercive economic and political
relationships are taken for granted, all of which are contrary to the
love-absolutism of the Gospels, cannot arbitrarily introduce the
uncompromising ethic of the Gospel into one particular issue". This
probably is the most difficult of all arguments for the average pacifist
to meet. For, unless we are prepared to contract out of organized
society, it is difficult enough to show why war is more offensive to
the Christian conscience than any other corporate evil; and, if we
discriminate against it, we may well involve ourselves in a charge of
inconsistency, if not of hypocrisy. This is a formidable indictment
which must be frankly faced and answered.

The Basic Fact of Human Sin

Niebuhr builds his own case for Christian non-pacifism on the
basic fact of human sin. "Christianity is a religion which measures
the total dimension of human existence not only in terms of the final
norm of human conduct, which is expressed in the law of love, but
also in terms of the fact of sin.[5] . . . The Gospel is something more
than the law of love".[6] When orthodox doctrine is reinterpreted in
the light of modern psychological science we see that original sin
"is not an inherited corruption, but it is an inevitable fact of human

[1] *An Interpretation of Christian Ethics*, 196 f.
[2] *Why the Christian Church is Not Pacifist*, 26.
[3] *An Interpretation of Christian Ethics*, 172.
[4] *Why the Christian Church is Not Pacifist*, 19 f.
[5] *Why the Christian Church is Not Pacifist*, 8.   [6] Ibid., 27.

existence".[1] Thus pacifist perfectionism is so much out of touch with human experience that "there are no historical realities which remotely conform to it".[2] This inherent sinfulness of human nature expresses itself above all in a "will-to-live" which, when it becomes accentuated, develops into a "will-to-power". Both these impulses are diametrically opposed to Jesus' ethic, which finds a man's fullest self-attainment in a willingness to "lose his life", and insists that the way of greatness is the way of humble service. Thus, even though we know that we can become our true selves only by striving for self-realization beyond ourselves, we are inevitably involved in making our own narrow selves the chief end of existence. There is an insuperable contradiction within our own souls: though we know we ought to love our neighbours as ourselves, there is "a law in our members which wars against the law that is in our mind", so that in fact we love first and foremost our own selves.

The Impossibility of the Ideal

Thus, even for the most Christ-like individual, loyalty to the way of Christ must mean only "realization in intention, but does not actually mean the full realization of the measure of Christ".[3] And if this be true of the Christian individual, much more it is true of social, political and national groups. For it is one of Niebuhr's postulates that "human collectives are less moral than the individuals which compose them".[4] "Human finiteness and sin are revealed with particular force in collective relationships" and "the full evil of human finitude and sin is most vividly revealed in conflicts between national communities".[5] Who, looking at the world today, would deny that "the evil impulses in men may be compounded in collective actions until they reach diabolical proportions"?[6] What possible relevance can an absolute perfectionist ethic have in such a world?

Grace as Pardon rather than as Power

If we argue that the grace of God in Jesus Christ can make possible what is beyond the power of unregenerate human nature, and that in the Church we have a "collective" or social fellowship in which the Holy Spirit should be active and powerful in a measure granted to no one individual, Niebuhr would reply somewhat as follows. Certainly the grace of God is regarded by Christian faith as an actual "power of righteousness" healing the contradiction

[1] An Interpretation of Christian Ethics, 100
[2] Why the Christian Church is Not Pacifist, 12
[3] Why the Christian Church is Not Pacifist, 9.
[4] An Interpretation of Christian Ethics, 134.   [5] Ibid., 136.   [6] Ibid., 26.

within our hearts. But "the question is whether the grace of Christ is primarily a power of righteousness which so heals the sinful heart that henceforth it is able to fulfil the law of love; or whether it is primarily the assurance of divine mercy for a persistent sinfulness".[1] Is the emphasis on sanctification or on justification? Niebuhr holds that in the New Testament "grace is conceived as justification, as pardon rather than as power, as the forgiveness of God which is vouchsafed to man despite the fact that he never achieves the full measure of Christ".[2]

The Justification of Force and of War

Niebuhr then draws his conclusions against Christian pacifism. Pacifists "do not see that sin introduces an element of conflict into the world, and that even the most loving relations are not free of it. . . . It is because men are sinners that justice can be achieved only by a certain degree of coercion on the one hand, and by resistance to coercion and tyranny on the other hand".[3] It is impossible to build a social or international order on the ideal of love alone, because that ideal presupposes the resolution of the very conflict of life with life and group with group which it is the concern of a just order to mitigate and restrain. Such an order is always dependent in the last resort on various "balances of power", and "a balance of power is something different from, and inferior to, the harmony of love. But it is a basic condition of justice, given the sinfulness of man".[4] It is on these grounds that under certain conditions even war may be justified: "Given the fact of sin, all justice in the realm of man's collective behaviour is achieved by securing some kind of decent equilibrium of power. But every such equilibrium stands under the peril of either tyranny or anarchy. Such a war as this one is merely the consequence of, and remedy for, the tyranny which results from irresponsible power. . . . If we are challenged to justify our participation in war in terms of our Christian faith, our answer is quite simply that we do not regard Christianity as a religion which merely preaches the simple moral injunction that men ought to love one another. Rather it is a religion which illumines the tragic fact that, though love is the law of life, no man completely lives by that law".[5]

The Tension between the Historical and the Transcendent

To what extent then is Jesus' absolute ethic relevant to the practical affairs of life? According to Niebuhr the ethical fruitfulness

[1] *Why the Christian Church is Not Pacifist*, 28.   [2] Ibid., 9.   [3] Ibid., 23.
[4] *Why the Christian Church is Not Pacifist*, 38.
[5] *The Christian News Letter*, Supplement No. 11.

of any religion depends on the extent to which it creates a "tension between the historical and the transcendent"; that is to say, there must be an awareness of the contradiction between what we are now and what we shall be when God's eternal purpose for us is fulfilled. In order that this tension may be maintained, on the one hand the ideal must be seen to transcend every possible achievement in the realm of history; on the other hand the transcendent and the historical must constantly be set side by side, so that the relevance of the ideal to actual life is not overlooked. Both orthodox and liberal Christianity have been guilty of relaxing this tension and thereby destroying the fruitfulness of the Christian ethic. Orthodoxy has done so by neglecting the relevance of the ideal of love to the ordinary problems of existence, because it is "certain that the tragedy of human life must be resolved by something more than moral achievement";[1] liberal Christianity in general, and pacifism in particular, has done so by claiming that through the practice of an absolute ethic the transcendent ideal can be realized in an immediate historical situation. Or to put this into concrete language: "The orthodox Church dismissed the immediate relevancy of the law of love for politics. The modern Church declared it to be relevant without qualification, and insisted upon the direct application of the Sermon on the Mount to the problems of politics and economics as the only way of salvation for a sick society".[2] Orthodoxy has led to complacency, liberalism to a naïve Utopianism. In either case the original and fruitful tension of the Christian ethic has been destroyed; but pacifism is the more guilty because for it "the transcendent impossibilities of the Christian ethic of love" have become "the immanent and imminent possibilities of an historical process".[3] Accordingly "if the relevance of the love commandment must be asserted against Christian orthodoxy, the impossibility of the ideal must be insisted upon against all those forms of liberalism which generate Utopian illusions and regard the love commandment as ultimately realizable".[4]

The Relevance of an Impossible Ideal

What relevance then has this impossible ethical ideal? Clearly it is not immediately applicable to social and international problems. It was framed for the Kingdom of God, which is a divine reality and not a human possibility. Probably Jesus Himself never thought of it as practicable, even in the world as He knew it; and, even if He did, it does not follow that it is practicable for us who are "involved in the relativities of politics, in resistance to tyranny or in social

---

[1] *An Interpretation of Christian Ethics*, 114.   [2] Ibid., 179.
[3] *An Interpretation of Christian Ethics*, 21.   [4] Ibid., 129.

conflict"[1] as Jesus Himself never was. Moreover this ethic of the Kingdom is one in which "no concession is made to human sin",[2] and in which "there is no advice on how we may hold the world of sin in check until the coming of the Kingdom of God".[3] It demands an absolute obedience to the will of God without consideration of any of the consequences of trying to practise a perfectionist ethic in an imperfect world. "It does not establish a connection with the horizontal points of a political or social ethic, or with the diagonals which a prudential individual ethic draws between the moral ideal and the facts of a given situation. It has only a vertical dimension between the loving will of God and the will of man".[4] And yet this ethic does, within strict limits, have a real relevance to every sphere of life.

(a) As the Measure of our Failure

Firstly, it provides us with an ideal standard against which we may measure the magnitude of our failure. Christianity demands the impossible, and by that very demand it emphasizes the impotence of human nature. "Some transcendent possibility always stands above every actuality, as a vantage point from which actual achievements are found wanting. Thus the ideal of perfect love gives a perspective upon every human action which prompts the confession, Are we not all unprofitable servants?"[5] Men are saved not by achieving perfection, but by the recognition of their inability to do so. "Individuals may be saved by repentance, which is the gateway to grace".[6]

(b) As the Ultimate Criterion of our Achievements

Secondly, the ideal law of love provides us with "an indiscriminate principle of criticism over all attempts at social and international justice";[7] that is to say it presents the absolute standard, the ultimate criterion, by which every attempt to create a new and better world must be judged. "The ultimate principles of the Kingdom of God are never irrelevant to any problem of justice, and they hover over every situation as an ideal possibility".[8] Though as a transcendent ideal the ethic of Jesus can itself provide no practicable way of life for a sinful world, nevertheless it "may offer valuable insights to and sources of criticism for a prudential social ethic which deals with present realities".[9] It is thus the best of all

[1]*Why the Christian Church is Not Pacifist*, 16.   [2]*Ibid.*, 19.
[3]*An Interpretation of Christian Ethics*, 61.
[4]*An Interpretation of Christian Ethics*, 49.   [5]*Ibid.*, 92.   [6]*Ibid.*, 99.
[7]*Why the Christian Church is Not Pacifist*, 33.
[8]*Why the Christian Church is Not Pacifist*, 36.
[9]*An Interpretation of Christian Ethics*, 61.

safeguards against complacency. "Against all forms of moral complacency the Christian faith must sharpen the sense of the Kingdom of God as a relevant alternative to every scheme and structure of human justice. It sees history as a realm of infinite possibilities. No limit can be placed upon the higher possibilities of justice which may be achieved in any given historic situation".[1] If Jesus' ethic can never become the way of life for a sinful humanity it can at least help us to set all our poor tentative experiments under the criticism of the ultimate ideal; above all "the law of love remains a principle of criticism over all forms of community in which elements of coercion and conflict destroy the highest type of fellowship".[2]

(c) As a Principle of Discriminate Criticism

Thirdly, and for Niebuhr this is of paramount importance, "the ideal of love is not merely a principle of indiscriminate criticism upon all approximations of justice. It is also a principle of discriminate criticism between forms of justice".[3] That is to say, when there are two or more alternatives, both admittedly falling short of the ideal, the law of love provides the criterion by which we may determine which of these several "second-bests" approximates most closely to the ideal. It may even lay upon us the duty of accepting what, in the light of the ideal, is obviously the lesser of two *evils*—for example, according to Niebuhr, war rather than submission to tyranny. Niebuhr's charge against Christian pacifism is that, in its mistaken striving after the absolute ideal, it refuses to make such discriminate judgments and face up to such discriminate choices. "If we do not make discriminate judgments between social systems we weaken the resolution to defend and extend civilization. Pacifism either tempts us to make no judgments at all, or to give an undue preference to tyranny in comparison with the momentary anarchy which is necessary to overcome tyranny".[4]

There follow from all this several very important practical conclusions.

"Equal Justice"

Firstly, given a sinful world and the impracticability of the way of absolute love, the nearest approximation to the ideal is to be found in "equal justice". It is admitted that such justice is a "second-best" which in the Kingdom of God would be transcended and "fulfilled" in the law of love. "The principles of equal justice

[1] *The Christian News Letter*, Supplement No. 16.
[2] *Why the Christian Church is Not Pacifist*, 33.
[3] *Why the Christian Church is Not Pacifist*, 33.   [4] Ibid., 41.

are approximations of the law of love in the kind of imperfect world which we know, and not principles which belong to a world of transcendent perfection".[1] Yet these principles are our only practicable guide to conduct in the common relationships of life.

The Necessity of Relative Judgments

Secondly, in order to attain even to this approximation to the ideal, we must be prepared to make relative judgments, that is, to discriminate between alternative "second-bests", to choose "the lesser of two evils", and with a good conscience to act upon such choices. "The relativity of all moral ideals cannot absolve us of the necessity and duty of choosing between relative values; and the choice is sometimes so clear as to become an imperative one".[2] Niebuhr's complaint against Christian pacifists is that they refuse to make these relative judgments. If Christian morality is "senseless when . . . it seeks uncritically to identify the cause of Christ with the cause of democracy, it is just as senseless when it purges itself of this error by an uncritical refusal to make any distinction between relative values in history."[3]

The Duty of Fighting for the Juster Cause

Thirdly, the ultimate standard of the Christian ideal "ought to persuade us that political controversies are always conflicts between sinners and not between righteous men and sinners".[4] But the fact that we ourselves are sinners, and that our own sin is always partly the cause of the evil by which we are confronted, must not be taken as proof that we have no right to resist that evil. If we imagine that "we have no right to act against an acknowledged evil because we are not ourselves pure, we are delivered into historic futility".[5] Once again we must exercise discriminate judgment between relative values and give our devotion to whatever cause seems most likely to achieve the highest measure of relative justice. For example "the fact that the evil incarnated in the Nazi state is the culminating expression of forms of cultural and social decay which are rife among ourselves, does not absolve us from the task of opposing that evil".[6] The truth is that "the Christian is freed by grace to act in history; to give his devotion to the highest values he knows" even though "he is persuaded by that grace to remember the ambiguity of even his best actions".[7]

[1] *An Interpretation of Christian Ethics*, 159.   [2] Ibid., 142.
[3] *Why the Christian Church is Not Pacifist*, 43.
[4] *Why the Christian Church is Not Pacifist*, 34.
[5] *The Christian News Letter*, Supplement No. 11.
[6] Ibid., Supplement No. 16.
[7] *Why the Christian Church is Not Pacifist*, 44.

The Tragic Results of Pacifism

Niebuhr finally insists that a failure to recognize these principles will inevitably result in moral anarchy both for the individual life and also in social and international relationships. In the case of the individual "the same man who touches the fringes of the infinite in his moral life remains imbedded in finiteness, and he increases the evil in his life if he tries to overcome it without regard to his limitations".[1] And as for international affairs: "It may yet be proved that the greatest tragedy of the present war is that Nazi tyranny was allowed to grow until it reached unparalleled proportions, precisely because so many citizens of a Christian civilization were prevented by these (pacifist) scruples from resisting the monster when there was yet time. If this should be true it would be 'tragic' in the narrow and exact sense of the word. It would reveal the possibility of evil emerging from our highest good".[2]

---

[1] *An Interpretation of Christian Ethics*, 145.
[2] *The Christian News Letter*, Supplement No. 11.

CHAPTER TWO

SOME CONCESSIONS TO PACIFISM

BEFORE attempting a constructive reply to Niebuhr's arguments it will be well to notice the very significant concessions which he makes to the pacifist position.

Firstly, there can be no question that the teaching of Jesus, if taken at its face value, is uncompromisingly pacifist. Niebuhr has no patience with those Christian theologians and ecclesiastics who still seek to discover loopholes through which war may be actually brought within the pale of Christian ethics and blessed in the name of the Prince of Peace: "It is very foolish to deny that the ethic of Jesus is an absolute and uncompromising ethic. . . . The injunctions 'resist not evil', 'love your enemies', . . . 'be not anxious for your life', 'be ye therefore perfect even as your Father in heaven is perfect', are all of one piece, and they are all uncompromising and absolute".[1] In the world as it is, forces over which we have no control may drive our nation into a war which appears as the lesser of two evils; but, when Christians take up arms, there is nothing in either the teaching or example of Jesus which would justify us in pointing to Him as our precedent: "Nothing is more futile and pathetic than the effort of some Christian theologians who find it necessary to become involved in the relativities of politics, in resistance to tyranny or in social conflict, to justify themselves by seeking to prove that Christ was also involved in some of these relativities, that He used whips to drive the money changers out of the Temple, or that He came 'not to bring peace but a sword', or that He asked the disciples to 'sell a cloak and buy a sword'."[2] The necessity of making "relative judgments" may drive us to compromise, but that does not alter the essentially uncompromising nature of Jesus' commands: "Those of us who regard the ethic of Jesus as finally and ultimately normative, but as not immediately applicable to the task of securing justice in a sinful world, are very foolish if we try to reduce the ethic so that it will cover and justify our prudential and relative standards and strategies".[3]

In other words, the debate between pacifist and non-pacifist ought to be not concerning any possible ambiguity in Jesus' teach-

[1] *Why the Christian Church is Not Pacifist*, 15.
[2] *Why the Christian Church is Not Pacifist*, 16.　　[3] Ibid., 16.

ing, which should be admitted to be unequivocally pacifist, but rather concerning its practicability, its relevance to present circumstances, the extent to which even Jesus Himself intended it to be put into effect in an imperfect world. The question is not, "Does Jesus command this?" but rather, "Does He mean us to obey what appears to be a plain command, and will He give us power to do so?" If the question was always as clearly posed as it is by Niebuhr, one feels that for most Christians, the debate would be closed.

Love as the Law of Life

Secondly, Niebuhr concedes that "pacifists are quite right in one emphasis. They are right in asserting that love is really the law of life".[1] Such "*agape*" (to use the Greek word for which there is no real English equivalent) is for most of us an emotion so vague, so diffuse, so inarticulate as to appear little more than pious sentimentality. Yet in times of stress it shows itself to be the chief motivating power of responsible human action, and the one secret of social cohesion. Why, for example, does some great natural catastrophe always evoke an outpouring of sympathy and generosity which oversteps all national boundaries? Such universal sympathy "can express itself, even in those rare moments, only because all human life is informed with an inchoate sense of responsibility toward the ultimate law of life—the law of love".[2]

Nor is this law merely a transcendental ideal; Jesus' ethic of love "is drawn from, and relevant to, every moral experience. It is immament in life as God is immament in the world".[3] It is commonly argued that Christ's law of love can be expected to operate only among those who have already accepted the presuppositions of the Christian Gospel. That, I take it, was Archbishop Temple's meaning when he wrote that "man is incapable of living by love unless the grace of God has both converted and sanctified him; so that the law of love is not applicable to nations consisting in large measure of unconverted or . . . very imperfectly converted citizens".[4] Niebuhr, on the contrary, rightly insists on the "relevance of the ideal of love to the moral experience of mankind on every conceivable level. It is not an ideal magically superimposed upon life by a revelation which has no relation to total human experience".[5] The compulsion of the love-commandment is as all-embracing as the love of God itself for men. "The Christian love-commandment does not demand love of the fellow-man because he

[1]*Why the Christian Church is Not Pacifist*, 32.
[2]*An Interpretation of Christian Ethics*, 123.   [3]Ibid., 47.
[4]York Diocesan Leaflet, 1935.
[5]*An Interpretation of Christian Ethics*, 114.

is with us equally divine, or because we ought to have 'respect for personality', but because God loves him".[1] All pacifists will feel that in writing thus Niebuhr has done much to build the bridge which must ultimately reunite pacifist and non-pacifist Christians.

The Place of the Pacifist in the Church

Finally, while pronouncing much pacifist doctrine to be "heretical", Niebuhr allows that there is a certain value in pacifism and a real place for pacifists in the Church. Modern Christian pacifism "expresses a genuine impulse in the heart of Christianity, the impulse to take the law of Christ seriously and not to allow the political strategies, which the sinful character of man makes necessary, to become final norms".[2] Such Christian perfectionism, provided that it limits itself to "the effort to achieve a standard of perfect love in individual life", need not come under the ban: it does so only when it regards the law of love "as an alternative to the political strategies by which the world achieves a precarious justice".[3] But when it relegates itself judiciously to its own sphere, and when "the political problem and task are specifically disavowed", this kind of pacifism is "not a heresy. It is rather a valuable asset for the Christian faith".[4] It may seem here—to use Niebuhr's own criticism of Brunner—that our author touches his cap to pacifism only at the cost of "neatly dismissing the Christian ideal from any immediate relevance to political issues",[5] Nevertheless he freely concedes that "religious pacifism, as a . . . symbolic portrayal of love absolutism in a sinful world, has its own value and justification. A Church which does not generate it is the poorer for its lack".[6] He would agree with Archbishop Temple (*pace* the Dean of St. Paul's!) that "pacifism is a genuine vocation for some"—though apparently not for Archbishops and Deans!

The Peril of Compromising with the Absolute

On the immediate problem of the Church's attitude to war in general, and this war in particular, Niebuhr utters two warnings to which Christian pacifists will give an emphatic "Amen!" Firstly, there is the peril of compromising with the absolute, particularly in the Church's relations with the State. It engulfed the Church in her early years: "When the hope of the *parousia* waned, the rigour of the Christian ethic was gradually dissipated and the Church, forced to come to terms with the relativities of politics and economics and the immediate necessities of life, made unnecessary compromises

---

[1]Ibid., 223.   [2]*Why the Christian Church is Not Pacifist*, 10.   [3]Ibid., 11.
[4]Ibid., 11.   [5]*An Interpretation of Christian Ethics*, 167.   [6]Ibid., 198.

with these relativities which frequently imperilled the very genius of prophetic religion".[1] Protestant tradition has given the State "special sanctification as an ordinance of God",[2] and the Lutheran doctrine of the two "domains" has resulted too often in an unwillingness on the part of the Church to apply to the State's actions, within the sphere of the latter's own domain, the critical sanctions of a Christian morality which was held to function only within the "order of grace". Yet, says Niebuhr, "it must also be noted that the Church usually capitulated in the end to the lower standards which it failed to challenge in the State".[3] So today the way of least resistance for the Church is to renounce all criticism of the State, so long as it acts strictly within its own domain, and (like the German Confessional Church) to protest in the name of Christ only when the State claims not only "the things that are Caesar's" but also "the things that are God's". Yet, says Niebuhr again, "a Church which refrains from practically every moral criticism of the State, and allows itself only an ultimate religious criticism of the spiritual pretensions of the State, must logically end in the plight in which the German Church finds itself".[4]

The Invocation of Religion in Support of War

Secondly, Niebuhr warns us against the tragic results of invoking religion in support of a national war effort. There has never been a war in which it has not been found necessary to buttress national morale by appealing to the religious instinct. "All wars are religious wars, whether fought in the name of historic creeds or not. Men do not fight for causes until they are 'religiously' devoted to them; which means not until the cause seems to them the centre of their universe of meaning. This is just as true in a supposedly secular age as in an avowedly religious one".[5] The result has been a vast amount of national hypocrisy and self-deception, as was only too evident in the last war: "A re-reading of the pronouncements of the men of learning and philosophers . . . who were involved in the world war fills the reader with a depressing sense of the calculated insincerity of all their pretensions. Yet while some of the sentiments were no doubt brazenly insincere and calculated to deceive the public, many of them were *merely a striking revelation of the pathos of modern spirituality*" (italics mine).[6]

Worst of all the constant invocation of religion produces a mood of national self-righteousness, which at the moment is perhaps the least admirable feature of our own national temper. The very fact that, at least in our own eyes, our cause is so obviously righteous

[1] *An Interpretation of Christian Ethics*, 69.   [2] Ibid., 164.   [3] Ibid., 156.
[4] *An Interpretation of Christian Ethics*, 171.   [5] Ibid., 244.   [6] Ibid., 234

sorely tempts us to identify our cause with God's and our victory with the triumph of God's Kingdom. God grant that it may indeed be so! Yet, warns Niebuhr, in all international disputes "every appeal to moral standards degenerates into a moral justification of the self against the enemy. Parties to a dispute inevitably make themselves judges over it and thus fall into the sin of pretending to be God. . . ."[1] The introduction of religious motives into these conflicts is usually no more than the final and most demonic pretension. Religion may be regarded as the last and final effort of the human spirit to escape relativity and gain a vantage point in the eternal".[2] One need not for one moment question the essential justice of the Allied cause in order to see that here the Church must ever be on her guard. Surely even those who are most convinced that Christianity today stands or falls with the British Empire will acknowledge the real peril to true religion latent in this (as Niebuhr calls it) "religious sanctification of partial and relative values".[3] To guard against it is one of the Church's primary tasks today, and we are grateful to Niebuhr for so clearly sounding the alarm.

It is encouraging that so keen an opponent of Christian pacifism as Niebuhr yet finds himself wholly at one with us over so large a portion of the field. Indeed one is conscious of a growing wonder that, starting from such presuppositions, our author can on the main issue of pacifism reach the conclusion set forth in his booklet.

---

[1] *An Interpretation of Christian Ethics*, 136.   [2] Ibid., 137.   [3] Ibid., 244

CHAPTER THREE

MAN, THE CHURCH AND THE HOLY SPIRIT

WE must now deal with the two main theological foundations of Niebuhr's position, leaving till later the criticism of the practical superstructure which he builds upon them. One—and this is the starting-point of his whole argument—is his doctrine of human depravity; the other is his view that Jesus' teaching envisages a Kingdom of God wholly transcendent and future, and that His perfectionist ethic therefore has no immediate relevance (save as an ideal standard and a principle of "discriminate criticism") to the practical problems of today. The first, I shall argue, springs from a quite unscriptural view of human nature; the second from a failure to grasp the really characteristic and essential elements in Jesus' teaching concerning the Kingdom of God. On purely rational grounds Niebuhr's case appears exceedingly formidable. But when examined in the light of the New Testament it is seen to be quite inconsistent with any but a badly maimed doctrine alike of the Incarnation, the Church, the Holy Spirit, the Cross, and the Kingdom of God.

Niebuhr's View of Human Nature

First, then, argues Niebuhr, man is so corrupted by sin as to be incapable, even if he would, of the sublimation of his selfish and antisocial instincts which obedience to the ethic of Jesus would demand. Between the "perfect" Father in heaven, to whom Jesus points as our exemplar, and the sinful creature which is man there is a gulf fixed which no striving after a perfectionist ideal can ever bridge. Man as a slave of sin is incapacitated from co-operating with God in the building of His Kingdom, a Kingdom which cannot be advanced by any human endeavour, but will come only when human history is wound up by an apocalyptic act of God. Here Niebuhr is, of course, much influenced by the transcendental theology of Karl Barth; and, over against the facile and shallow humanism of yesterday, Barth has supplied a much-needed corrective. Complacency and self-sufficiency *is* man's fundamental sin; the confession that "our righteousnesses are as filthy rags" is the first condition of his forgiveness; the denial of the reality and power of evil is his final apostasy. All that Barth and his school have to say about the nothingness and sinfulness of man before God is true. But is it the whole truth? If the world is indeed a sink of iniquity for which there is no hope of progress within the span of history; if all striving towards the Kingdom of God is mere unregenerate arrogance; then clearly the pacifist renunciation of war as a step in such progress is little short of blasphemous presumption.

Is it the View of the Gospels?

But the Gospels give us a very different picture. So far from teaching that God is "wholly other" than His world and His creatures, Jesus saw the world always and everywhere as God's world. He drew His lessons from birds and flowers, from the processes of growth and the handiwork of men; and when He wished to teach us what God is like He pointed to the God-like in men. Even in the worst sinner He could discover the hidden good and appeal to it, knowing that the good and not the evil is the essential man. He tells us that it is when a sinner "comes to himself" that he "arises and goes to his Father": the truly human in man, the man's true self, is that within him which responds to God. One little parable, that of the "Seed Growing Secretly", seems to suggest that the very nature of the world, so far from thwarting God's purposes, fosters their growth. Whatever mischances may befall God's Word, nature itself, if left to itself, is on God's side. Indeed to the Jesus of the Gospels the whole world is plainly sacramental. He is amazed that men are so blind to the care and presence of a Father God in His own world and to the "signs of the times" in all that befalls it. This faith in an ever-present Father never blinds Jesus to the reality of sin or to the eternal warfare between light and darkness. Yet He believes that, if a man will but "lose his life" in order to "find it", then God's will can "be done *in earth* as it is in heaven"—even though that will may prove to be a cross.

And is it Paul's View?

Now this teaching concerning the kinship of God's world with Himself is clearly Jesus' own. It can hardly have been imposed upon Him by a later age, the trend of whose thought was all in the other direction, towards the same kind of pessimistic dualism which is rampant today. Therefore the Gospels must be taken as normative, even if Paul should at first sight appear to give us a different estimate of human nature. But, rightly understood, Paul only corroborates Jesus. Here I cannot do better than quote C. E. Raven: "If St. Paul's view of nature had been the unrelieved and total condemnation which Paulinism has often ascribed to it, the power and poignancy of his teaching would have been impossible. It is because creation is redeemable and redemption is offered to it, that its continuance in sin becomes an outrage that cannot be tolerated. . . . Depraved as the world is, Christ's coming has revealed it to be in some measure *capax deitatis*, able to respond to and co-operate with His purposes, endowed by virtue of His creating and sustaining relationship to it with a value which makes the dominion of evil all the more detestable but which evil cannot utterly eradicate. . . . If the Pauline claims are true, then there is always and everywhere a relationship, a gracious, personal relationship, between God and His creation. This does not for sinner or saint imply perfection or minimize responsibility. . . . But it excludes the type of theology which rigidly sunders the natural from the redeemed, regards the world as a mass of corruption, and treats Christ as a divine intruder rescuing out of a wholly estranged and otherwise godless universe those who are elected to receive His salvation. . . . Creation is redeemable in virtue of its relatedness to Christ as its source and of His will to redeem it".[1]

A true "Theology of Crisis"

The estimate of human nature on which Niebuhr's case so largely depends is one of pessimism and gloom entirely out of tune with the joy and hope of the whole New Testament. It seriously distorts the New Testament doctrine of the Incarnation, for it makes Christ's nature exclusive rather than representative, and sees Him as a "divine intruder" into an alien world rather than as "the first-born of all creation". It gives little or no meaning, as we shall see, to the Holy Spirit; and it makes nonsense of Paul's claim that "we are fellow-workers together with God". It is fair to remember that it was the last war which, in the Barthian "theology of crisis", gave a fresh leash of life to this reactionary theology of despair for which there is no justification either in Scripture or in the Christian creed. Certainly the world's agony has taught us this much, that "progress" is not the easy, inevitable evolutionary process of which once we dreamed. As C. H. Dodd has said, "the Gospel does not speak of progress, but of dying and rising again. The pattern of history is revealed less in evolution than in crisis".[2] But a true theology of the present crisis will point us along another road than Barth's—"not to a denunciation of secular effort as irrelevant, nor to the acceptance of a godless and irredeemable State over against a pietistic and other-worldly Church, but to an insistence that no sphere of human activity is or can be purely secular, and that everywhere there is

[1] C. E. Raven, *The Gospel and the Church*, 40-42.
[2] *The Apostolic Preaching*, 238.

need for penitence and faith, since all things secular and sacred work together for good to them that love God, and will work only for disaster on any other terms".[1]

"Immoral Society" and the Doctrine of the Church

But, if it is possible for the redeemed Christian individual to co-operate with God in the achievement of His perfect will, is it any less possible for a redeemed fellowship, in this case for the Christian Church? For it is fair to remind Niebuhr that by his own definition the question at issue is "Why the *Christian Church* is not Pacifist". It is Niebuhr's thesis that "human collectives are less moral than the individuals which compose them"[2] and that therefore there is a radical difference between personal and collective ethics. Now, the question of war apart, the average Christian would almost certainly repudiate the suggestion that he may legitimately live by one set of principles as an individual and by another as a citizen. Dean Inge calls this idea "that ruinous dualism of public and private ethics . . . which by openly proclaiming that the teaching of Christ has no reference to the conduct of States has made modern Europe a hell upon earth".[3] Yet this assumption underlies practically every statement of the Christian non-pacifist position. But is this thesis of "moral man and immoral society" really tenable on Christian grounds? Surely it is questionable even with respect to ordinary secular society. No doubt there is a superficial truth in the view that the group mind tends to revert towards the primitive and the savage, and that the morality of the crowd falls below that of the individual. But a group can rise above the sum of its members, as well as fall below it. There is an inspiration in fellowship which enables comrades to rise to levels impossible to the mere individual. *Esprit de corps* raises and does not lower morale! But the needful condition is inspiration by a common enthusiasm and a common purpose. It is this that distinguishes a fellowship from a mob; and though Niebuhr's thesis may be true of a mob it is emphatically not true of a fellowship. And the classic example of the fulfilment of such a condition is the Christian Church "continuing steadfastly of one accord" at Pentecost. We must return later to the inevitable conflict of loyalties which arises for the Christian in virtue of his membership both in a Christian communion and in a semi-Christian or non-Christian community. Suffice it for the moment to remark that Niebuhr's thesis is flatly irreconcilable with the Christian's faith in the Church and his own experience of *koinonia* in that Church. Indeed Niebuhr in his whole argument, and specially at this point,

[1]Raven, *op. cit.*, 221.   [2]*An Interpretation of Christian Ethics*, 134.
[3]*The Fall of the Idols*, 179.

seems practically to ignore the whole New Testament doctrine of
the Church, and the implications for the Christian of his membership of the Church—literally as a member or limb of the Body of
Christ. Can it really be true that such a Body as a whole is so sunk
in depravity, and so nerveless through the ravages of sin, that it
cannot co-operate with God in the doing of His perfect will? Has
the absolute ethic of Jesus really no more immediate relevance to
such a Body than is recognized by the rival leaders of warring
States? Again we remind ourselves that our problem is, "Why the
Christian Church is not Pacifist".

The Holy Spirit and "Enabling Grace"

If Niebuhr's argument does injustice to the New Testament
doctrine of the Church, he has apparently no doctrine at all of the
Holy Spirit—at any rate in the New Testament sense. We have
already noted that he regards grace as pardon rather than as power:
he appears to have little conception at all of "enabling grace". Yet
to remove this doctrine from the New Testament is to tear out its
very heart. It is an essential part of Paul's faith; otherwise how can
he speak of "His power that worketh in me mightily",[1] or pray to
be "strengthened with might by His spirit in the inner man",[2] or
boast that "I can do all things through Christ which strengthened
me"?[3] As proof of man's powerlessness, even if he would, to obey
Jesus' commands Niebuhr lays much stress on Paul's own experience of inner conflict set up by the tension between the "law in my
members" and the "law of my mind", each warring against the
other.[4] "The good that I would I do not: but the evil that I would
not, that I do".[5] No man ever had a keener sense of the reality and
the power of sin. But surely he is describing here not, as Niebuhr
seems to suggest, a permanent disability which would render all
moral effort irrelevant, but rather his own desperate moral conflict
before he met Christ on the Damascus road. "The Gospel in Pauline
thought has a supreme regenerative value precisely because it frees
a man from this conflict, integrates and sublimates his personality,
and so releases in him the power, previously wasted over inward
friction, to adjust himself to his environment and gain the mastery
of circumstance. Henceforward he is no longer the 'slave of sin' . . .
but is free to live as the child of God in the fellowship of his
brethren".[6] For Paul every step towards the attainment of the
Christian ideal is a "fruit of the Spirit", that is a product of a new
life of which the Spirit is the author; and this new life is the first
result of the Christian's status "in Christ". "If any man be in Christ

[1]Col. i. 29.   [2]Eph. i. 16.   [3]Phil. iv. 13.   [4]Rom. vii. 23.   [5]Rom. vii. 19.
[6]Raven, *op. cit.*, 135.

there is a new creation": consequently "the servant of Christ is capable of a perfect obedience because he has been transformed in the very constitution of his being".[1] Henceforward the moral demands of the Christian ethic become "the law of the Spirit" and are spontaneously and joyfully obeyed. Moreover it is not in the individual but in the fellowship of the Church that the work of the Holy Spirit is most powerfully manifested. The supreme example of the communion of a Spirit-filled fellowship with God is seen in the Church at Pentecost; and the final purpose of the Holy Spirit's mission is the "perfecting of the saints . . . unto the building up of the Body of Christ . . . till we all attain unto a fullgrown man, unto the measure of the stature of the fullness of Christ".[2] That such is Paul's teaching—however incredible it may seem to our poor faith or in the light of our own experience of failure both as individuals and as a Church—there can be no shadow of doubt; and no treatment of Christian ethics can be adequate which does not take account of it.

[1] E. F. Scott, *The Spirit in the New Testament*, 140.   [2] Eph. iv. 12 f.

CHAPTER FOUR

THE KINGDOM OF GOD AND THE RELEVANCE OF THE ETHIC

Evading the Relevance of the Absolute Ethic

IN the second place Niebuhr argues that Jesus' perfectionist ethic, framed as it is in view of a wholly transcendent and future Kingdom of God, was never intended, possibly even by our Lord Himself, to be applicable to the imperfect world in which we live. Now there are many ways of evading the relevance of Jesus' absolute demands, so that they may not challenge traditional dogma or conflict with the dictates of prudence and expediency. There is the "eschatological" argument, according to which Jesus' teaching is merely an "interim-ethic" intended to bridge the brief gap between Jesus' own day and the breaking in of the quickly-expected transcendent Kingdom. But Jesus makes His characteristic demands not in view of an immediate end of the present age, but on the ground that such a way of life is alone consistent with His own conception of God's nature; and Jesus' view of God is surely, if anything is, a permanent and unchangeable element in His teaching. This indeed Niebuhr admits: "The note of apocalyptic urgency is significantly lacking in many of the passages in which the religio-ethical rigour is most uncompromising. The motive advanced for fulfilling the absolute demands is simply that of obedience to God or emulation of His nature, and there is no suggestion that the world should be held in contempt because it will soon pass away". And again: "The justification for these demands is put in purely religious . . . terms. We are to forgive because God forgives; we are to love our enemies because God is impartial in His love."[1]

Again there is the "sacred-secular" argument, by which occasionally Niebuhr seems to be attracted. Jesus, it runs, intended His rule of life to be practised only within the community of His own disciples, and never contemplated that it should be applied, even by Christians, in their contacts with the outside world. But the good Jew always insisted that his religion was coextensive with the whole of his life; and it is inconceivable that Jesus should formulate an ethic for a "religious" community without intending that its im-

[1] *An Interpretation of Christian Ethics*, 66, 56.

perative should extend into every practical relationship of life. If Niebuhr and his Barthian mentors really believed this, then, as Raven well puts it, "logically they ought to advocate a total with-drawal from the world of government or of production; for, if that world is necessarily outside the order of grace, the Christian can only live in it by accepting a dual allegiance. Actually they seem more willing to denounce all that has been done to christianize the social order, and unable to supply any sort of guidance as to Christian conduct in relation to it."[1]

Jesus and the "Relativities of Politics"

More integral to Niebuhr's case is the argument that Jesus was not to the slightest degree "involved in the relativities of politics",[2] and therefore His teaching has no immediate bearing upon the practical problems with which a Christian society is confronted today. This, I believe, is a complete misreading of the historical situation pictured in the Gospels. Jesus' words, even though their immediate reference is to the individual disciple, cannot be isolated from the actual social and political circumstances in which they were spoken. All His teaching must be read in the light of His claim to be Messiah; and to His fellow-countrymen the most striking thing about His Messiahship must have been His refusal to deal with the political situation as Messiah was expected to deal with it, by waging the Messianic war. He cannot have bidden men to "love their enemies" without being compelled by His questioners to relate such teaching to the actual political situation in an "occupied territory." As C. H. Dodd has vividly put it: "We should observe that the situation into which Jesus Christ came was genuinely typical. The forces with which He came into contact were such as are permanent factors in history: government (in Pilate and the Sanhedrin), institutional religion (in the Pharisees), nationalism (in the Zealots), social unrest (in the poor and dispossessed of Galilee). That is to say, they are the stuff of our own historical situation."[3] It is really incredible that Jesus as claimant to the Messiahship, could have ignored political problems, and the question of war in particular, as completely as some Christians like to believe, or could have failed to apply to them His own characteristic ethical principles. Indeed, as C. J. Cadoux has remarked, "The politics of Jesus were no mere incident or accident of His ministry; they were inter-woven with the most central things in His Gospel."[4]

[1] Op. cit., 222.
[2] Why the Christian Church is Not Pacifist, 16.
[3] The Christian News Letter, Supplement No. 31.
[4] Congregational Quarterly, January 1936.

Jesus' Teaching on the Kingdom of God

But Niebuhr's argument appears to leave quite out of account what are in fact the most essential and characteristic features of Jesus' teaching about the Kingdom of God. For Niebuhr, Jesus' "counsels of perfection" have no immediate relevance to "political relativities", because the Kingdom of God to which they are related is, even in the thought of Jesus Himself, wholly transcendent and wholly future. Now Niebuhr is stating a profound truth when he insists that the fruitfulness of all ethical teaching depends on its ability to maintain "a tension between the historical and the transcendent", the contrast between the imperfect present and the consummation which is God's perfect will. The function of the eschatological element in Jesus' teaching is precisely to maintain this tension. As Rudolph Otto puts it, all genuine eschatology includes two things: "There is the idea of the wondrous new creation. . . . In this idea lies the contrast between that which is yonder and that which is here. There is also the idea of its real coming, in which lies the contrast between the Future and the Present."[1] But the power of Jesus' teaching lies precisely at the point where it passes beyond conventional Jewish eschatology. In particular two characteristic features must be underlined. Both are thoroughly paradoxical, not to say irrational. But, as Otto says, it is "the irrationality of the genuine and typically eschatological attitude";[2] and it is this very irrationality which maintains the tension with which Niebuhr rightly is so concerned.

(a) *The Kingdom Transcendent, yet on Earth*

Firstly, the Kingdom though transcendent is yet to be manifested in this world. We are bidden by Jesus to pray "Thy Kingdom come; Thy will be done *in earth*, as it is in heaven." Earth no less than heaven is the sphere of God's Kingdom, where His will can and shall be done. That is to say, although this world is a fallen world, it is still God's world and "His Kingdom ruleth over all." In Christ it is God's will to redeem a sinful world order, and not to abolish this world by the coming of His "reign", as was the dream of apocalyptists. The obedient servant of His Kingdom must therefore be in the world, where alone the process of redemption may be carried on. When we pray "Thy Kingdom come in earth," we are not merely hoping that some day and somewhere God's Kingdom will become a reality; we are not regretfully postponing the Reign of God either to heaven or to Utopia. We are accepting it here and now; and the obligation laid upon us by that acceptance is binding

[1] *The Kingdom of God and the Son of Man*, p. 53.   [2] *Op. cit.*, 62.

here and now, even though we know that it cannot be completely fulfilled by men living in this world. Hence the "tension" of which we have spoken. And, as C. H. Dodd puts it, "in experiencing this tension we become 'fellow workers with God'; for the impact of the order of the Kingdom of God upon the secular order takes place in us and through us";[1] and again, "If our belief in the Kingdom of God is to be a living faith, and our prayer for it a prayer that expresses an urgent need, then *the Kingdom of God must be a reality accessible to us now, within history*."[2] As according to Niebuhr the whole of Jesus' ethic is conceived with direct reference to the Kingdom, to deny this is to reduce His teaching to so much apocalyptic day-dreaming. As G. J. Heering has pungently put it, "There is no more effective way of disabling the Gospel than first to relegate the fulfilment of Christ's commands to the Kingdom of God, and then to read His saying, My Kingdom is not *of* this world, as if He had said, My Kingdom is not *for* this world."[3]

(b) *The Kingdom Future, yet Present in Christ*

Secondly, though the Kingdom in its full consummation is still future, in numerous passages Jesus proclaims that with Himself that Kingdom, the hope of many generations, has at last come. "Many prophets and righteous men desired to see the things which ye see, and saw them not."[4] The Kingdom is not merely imminent; it is here. From this point of view Dodd has described the life and teaching of Jesus as "realized eschatology", that is to say, as the "impact upon this world of the powers of the world to come in a series of events, unprecedented and unrepeatable, now in actual process"; and he adds, "Whatever we make of them, the sayings which declare the Kingdom of God to have come are explicit and unequivocal. They are moreover the most characteristic and distinctive of the Gospel sayings on the subject. They have no parallel in Jewish teaching or prayers of the period. If therefore we are seeking the *differentia* of the teaching of Jesus upon the Kingdom of God, it is here that it must be found."[5]

Particularly characteristic is the idea that it is in Jesus' own person that the Kingdom has come, and that it manifests itself in a *divine power* to transform the world—a power which is already in operation. All the best recent work on the New Testament finds here the really characteristic feature of Jesus' teaching on the Kingdom. Particularly significant is the work of Rudolph Otto, all the more so

[1] *The Bases of Christian Pacifism*, p. 13.
[2] *Christian News Letter*, Supplement 31.
[3] *The Fall of Christianity*, p. 34.   [4] Matt. xiii. 17.
[5] *The Parables of the Kingdom*, 51, 49.

because in certain respects his theological outlook is similar to Niebuhr's own. Jesus, as he says, "ranged far beyond (the Jewish apocalyptists) by an idea which was entirely unique and peculiar to him, that the Kingdom—supramundane, future, and belonging to a new era—penetrated from the future into the present, from its place in the beyond into this order, and was operative redemptively as a divine *dynamis*, as an inbreaking realm of salvation." And again, "What distinguished Jesus' own eschatology from previous forms was . . . that he already lived in the miracle of the new age which was active even in the present; that with clear vision he saw this as something already developing and growing around himself; that he knew himself to be supported by powers which . . . were already penetrating the world, and supported and filled by these powers he worked and preached."[1]

The Kingdom Operative as Redeeming Power

Lack of space forbids lengthy illustration of this too often neglected aspect of Jesus' teaching. Suffice it to say that it is the main point of nearly all the Parables of the Kingdom in Mark iv. As B. W. Bacon has written, these parables "have a common object, to confirm the glad tidings of the coming kingdom as a power of God already at work. . . . The chief lesson is the present, inward working of God's Spirit, unseen by dull or hostile eyes, a kingdom of God which is already in the midst, silent, omnipotent, overtaking unawares those whose spiritual eyes are closed."[2]

Some of Jesus' greatest sayings point the same lesson—in His own person the Kingdom of God is breaking through upon earth. When the Seventy "returned with joy" Jesus cries out in triumph "I beheld Satan fallen as lightning from heaven."[3] His wonderful works are the guarantee of the coming of the Kingdom: "If I by the Spirit of God am casting out devils, then has the Kingdom of God actually come upon you."[4] That is to say, "His person and work were part of a comprehensive redemptive event, which broke in with Him and which He called the coming and actual arrival of the Kingdom of God."[5] And it is above all as saving power that Jesus thinks of the Kingdom as manifesting itself: "From the days of John until now the Kingdom of heaven is exercising its force" (*biazetai*, which almost certainly should be taken as an intensive middle. Matt. xi. 12). To sum up in Otto's own words: "The kingdom comes in and with him . . . in order that it may now become real 'in earth as it is in heaven.' And it comes chiefly . . . as

[1]*Op. cit.*, 72, 155.
[2]*The Story of Jesus and the Beginnings of the Church*, p. 212.
[3]Luke x. 18.   [4]Matt. xii. 28.   [5]Otto, *op. cit.*, 104.

redeeming power, to set free a world lying in the clutches of Satan, threatened by the devil and by demons, tormented, possessed, demon-ridden; and to capture the spoil from the strong one."[1] What a Gospel for today, if only we would take God at His word!

The Whole New Testament in Harmony with Jesus

Nor is this point of view confined to the sayings of Jesus in the Synoptic Gospels. St. John rightly interprets it both when he regularly pictures Jesus' mighty works as "signs" of the coming of "eternal life" to men, and when he transmutes the eschatology of the earlier Gospels into the doctrine of an already present and abiding "Comforter." Paul too does full justice to Jesus' proclamation of a present Kingdom when he teaches that, though the consummation of eternal life is still a future promise, the "earnest" of this inheritance is already a present possession;[2] for an "earnest" is a sample of goods which guarantees the main consignment to be of the same kind and quality. Finally the writer to the Hebrews clinches the matter when he tells us that in Christ we have already "tasted . . . the powers of the world to come."[3]

The Inference for the Church Today

To grasp this essential element in New Testament teaching does not indeed make any less agonizing the conflict of loyalties and choices in which the Christian is involved when he seeks to obey the laws of the Kingdom amidst the moral anarchy of a world at war. But it does sting him into consciousness of the obligation under which he stands. If Jesus really believed and taught that with His coming there had broken through from the transcendent kingdom a new divine power for the redemption and transformation of this present world, then it will not do for Christians to argue that for Jesus Himself the Kingdom was wholly otherworldly, and that therefore the ethic framed with a view to that Kingdom may be safely and honourably discounted in a world in which that Kingdom is still a future dream. Whatever be the conclusions of a prudential morality, that is clearly to evade both the intention of Jesus' teaching and the interpretation placed upon it by all the New Testament writers. Above all it is to shut our eyes to one adequate source of power for the world's salvation. If we have rightly interpreted the New Testament, then, as Dodd reminds us, "We are wrong in confining (the New Testament promises) to purely spiritual experience. They declare that as *any situation* is brought within the context of sacred history, with its creative centre in the Gospel facts,

---

[1]*Op. cit.*, 105.   [2]Eph. i. 14 ; 2 Cor. i. 22, v. 5.   [3]Heb. vi. 5.

it is exposed not only to the judgment of God, but also to possibilities of transformation and renewal which we can neither define nor limit, because they lie within the immeasurable power of the mercy of God. It is to this transformation of *an actual situation* that the prayer of the Church refers: Thy Kingdom come."[1]

To some of us the most tragic factor in the present catastrophe has been the Church's failure to use the power which, in Jesus Christ, God has placed in her hands, and which through the Church's obedience might have been released for the world's redemption. We Christian pacifists have often been warned by our "realist" friends that we cannot bring in the Kingdom of God by acting as if it were already here. Yet this is, I believe, precisely what Jesus *did* teach: if only men were prepared to take God at His word, and to order their lives here and now by the laws of a transcendent Kingdom, then the power of God would answer the cry of faith, and the Kingdom would break in upon them anew and "take them unawares." If Jesus were no more than a great teacher of ethics— possibly the world's greatest— then Niebuhr's case is unanswerable. But if He is indeed the Son of God? If the Church is His Body and we "members in particular"? If in His Word we have a unique revelation of God's will? If by His Spirit we are empowered for obedience?

[1]*History and the Gospel,* 176.

CHAPTER FIVE

WHY ISOLATE WAR?

WE are now in a position to relate what has been said more
immediately to the particular issue of war. Perhaps the
most damaging charge brought by Niebuhr against pacifists is that they unjustifiably isolate war from the ethical problem
as a whole—and this in two ways. Firstly, pacifists demand with
reference to this one moral issue an absolute obedience to the
perfectionist ethic, which they are not prepared to give over the
whole range of life; secondly, on this issue they are prepared to
separate themselves from the community of their fellow-citizens,
while continuing to claim the advantages accruing from membership of that community. The second point will come up again in
connection with the conflict of loyalties in which the Christian as a
member of a non-Christian society is inevitably involved. The first
point is best met by referring once again to that "tension between
the historical and the transcendent" on which Niebuhr himself
rightly lays such emphasis.

Where the "Tension" Reaches Breaking-point

The obligation laid upon us to accept the laws of the Kingdom is
absolute; yet, in a world not yet wholly redeemed, it can never be
completely fulfilled. Hence the "tension" of which we speak. Now
if this tension is indeed to contribute to ethical progress, then from
time to time it will become particularly acute at one point or
another. And this has, in fact, happened in history. Under the
guidance, we believe, of the Holy Spirit the Christian conscience
has become particularly sensitive upon one particular issue, because
it has seen there an eruption-point of the forces of evil in their
invasion of the Kingdom of God. And at that point Christians have
been driven to make a stand, even if that meant at least a temporary
withdrawal from solidarity with the community with respect to that
particular issue. So it was when the early Church felt compelled to
withdraw from collaboration with the State at every point where
idolatry was involved. As Dodd puts it: It was not that this was the
only thing in the Graeco-Roman world which was contrary to the
principles of the Kingdom of God; but this was the point at which
the opposition to the Kingdom of God seemed at the time to be

concentrated; and the Church drew the line firmly, not counting the cost of such non-co-operation."[1] Now the Christian pacifist believes that, at least since modern war revealed its true nature in the years 1914 to 1918, the crucial ethical question has been that of war. In it is concentrated everything that is fundamentally antagonistic to the principles of the Kingdom of God, and consequently it marks the point at which the tension between the worldly order and that transcendent Kingdom reaches the breaking-point, and where the Christian Church must make its final stand.

The Crucial Moral Issue for Today

Or to put the matter otherwise: the providence of God in history appears to bring about a series of moral crises in which some particular issue is presented to the Christian conscience for its judgment. One hundred and fifty years ago the issue was slavery, and Wilberforce supplies an extraordinarily significant illustration of this "step-by-step" method of reform. While striving untiringly for the liberation of negro slaves, he yet remained surprisingly blind to the contemporary enslavement at home of women and children by the new industrialism. Yet, by concentrating on the one issue, he established principles as to the infinite value of human personality, and the infinite sinfulness of its exploitation, that were quickly applied to the reform of other evils in society to which Wilberforce himself was blind. Now for twenty-five years pacifists have seen that for our own generation the fundamental moral issue has by sheer historical necessity come to be war. Other evils there are in society hardly less devilish; but at the moment they cannot be dealt with until the supreme evil of war is removed. The average Christian may hold in suspense his answer to the question whether war has ever been justifiable on Christian standards, or at exactly what point the use of force ceases to be ethical. But he sees clearly enough that in war as it has come to be we have passed far beyond that point, that war at this moment represents a concentration of everything which is most irreconcilably opposed to the will of God as shown in Christ. If war evokes almost incredible heroism and self-sacrifice, that does not redeem its essential evil; it only proves that even out of the worst evil the power of God in man can call forth virtue; and these splendid virtues war exploits in the service of hatred and death. Hence the inner compulsion which drives the Christian pacifist, even when bitterly conscious that he cannot disentangle himself from the sin of a non-Christian society of which he is part, to declare alike before his fellows and his own conscience, "Here I stand; so help me God; I can none other!"

[1] The Bases of Christian Pacifism, 13.

The "Step-by-Step" Method of Reform

Certainly this "step-by-step" method of reform has its own moral dangers. It suggests that the obligation of Christian discipleship can be satisfied by obedience in a few selected fields rather than through a radical repentance or "change of mind" covering the whole range of life—that we can get rid of "sin" piecemeal by renouncing in succession certain specific "sins." Yet it is obvious that Jesus Himself, while he made an absolute and unlimited demand upon those who would follow Him, yet graciously welcomed a discipleship which was in fact grievously imperfect. He did not refuse the crumbs because the whole loaf was not yet ready to be offered. The fact that we cannot reach perfection is hardly a sufficient reason for not striving to move towards it. Whatever be true of Professors of Applied Christianity, to the plain man it seems a strange argument that, because we have failed as yet to Christianize many corporate relationships, we ought therefore deliberately to support the diabolical antithesis of Christianity which war has come to be; that, because the Christian cannot wholly disentangle himself from all the evils of society, he does wrong to dissociate himself from the most flagrant evil of all. Niebuhr rightly warns us that the consciousness of being involved in the common sin of society does not absolve us from the duty of resisting what we see to be the greater evil. Surely then it follows from his own principles that we fail no less in duty if at the point of acute tension we fail to obey conscience and renounce evil, even though we know ourselves at other points still to be in its grip.

Renunciation of War only the First Step

No Christian pacifist will deny that war-refusal is merely emotional sentimentalism unless it becomes the focal point of his struggle against everything in the community which denies the Christian way of life. As the Fellowship of Reconciliation states in its Basis, we believe "that in order to establish a world-order based on love it is incumbent on those who believe in this principle to accept it fully, both for themselves and in their relation to others, and to take the risks involved in doing so in a world which does not accept it." We believe not only that "we are forbidden to wage war," but that "our loyalty to our country, to the Church Universal, and to Jesus Christ our Lord and Master, calls us instead to a life-service for the enthronement of Love in personal, social, commercial and national life." If war is singled out for special emphasis, it is only that for today war presents itself as the test case. It is still possible to hope that the Christian may best play his part in

Christianizing government, commerce and industry, the other activities of the present social order in spite of the evil inherent in them, by continuing to co-operate in them. No Christian, by his participation in it, can hope to Christianize war. Strangely enough, most thinking people outside the Churches are much quicker to realize this than are professing Christians. Thus a prominent left-wing journalist, who is a whole-hearted supporter of the country's present war-effort, writes: "Personally I was brought up in the Christian faith, and because I learnt what Christianity is I know now that I am not a Christian. . . . The only Christian victory is to persuade one's enemy. . . . If, failing to overcome evil by good or despairing to make the attempt, one decides not to turn the cheek but to choose good bombing targets and bomb them hard; if, instead of praying for them that despitefully use you, you pray on the contrary for victory, then your course may be right on national or rational or liberal or socialist or other principles, but it cannot be right on Christian principles. . . . We listen to Archbishops as we listen to politicians and agree or disagree on political grounds. When they try to relate what they say to the teaching of Christ, we blush. . . ."[1]

The Demand for "Relative Judgments"

Most characteristic of Niebuhr is his insistence that we must use Jesus' absolute ethic as a "principle of discriminate criticism" guiding us in our choice between relative values. He rightly reminds us that "the Christian faith ought to persuade us that political controversies are always controversies between sinners, and not between righteous men and sinners."[2] But where the absolute good is not within our reach we must be prepared to discriminate between alternative "second-bests", to choose the lesser "of two evils", and in consequence, even when neither cause is blameless, to defend the relatively juster of the two. "If we think that the moral and religious judgment, which discovers us all to be sinners in the sight of God, means that we have no right to act against an acknowledged evil because we are not ourselves pure, we are delivered into historic futility."[3] This, of course, is profoundly true, though Niebuhr himself admits that "national animosities might be appeased if nations could hear the accusing word, 'Let him who is without sin cast the first stone'; only a forgiving love, grounded in repentance, is adequate to heal the animosities of the nations."[4] We

[1]Kingsley Martin in a review of J. Middleton Murry's *The Betrayal of Christ by the Churches*.   [2]*Why the Christian Church is Not Pacifist*, 34.
[3]*The Christian News Letter*, Supplement, No. 11.
[4]*An Interpretation of Christian Ethics*, 139.

shall also insist that everything depends on *how* we "act against an acknowledged evil," or else we shall find ourselves committed to the position (to which indeed Niebuhr's argument leads dangerously near) that any evil thing may rightly be used as a remedy for anything more evil than itself. In the case of war at least three discriminate judgments seem to be called for: (*a*) Which is in fact the "juster cause"? (*b*) Does participation in war, or Niebuhr would put it, "capitulation to tyranny" involve the greater evil? (*c*) Which is to have over-riding authority—loyalty to the national State, which demands war, or loyalty to a Catholic Church, a universal brotherhood, a way of love, which just as clearly forbids it?

(a) *How Determine the Juster Cause?*

One may well question whether, once the passions of war are aroused, it is ever possible to reach on the issue of the "juster cause" an unbiassed relative judgment—at any rate one clear and compelling enough to justify action which otherwise would stand condemned by that same ethic which we are using as our "principle of discriminate criticism." Thus Niebuhr himself, writing in the relatively dispassionate days of 1936, admits that "if the issues are too confused to justify the hope of any solid gain for the cause of justice, abstention from the conflict may be the only possible course. Such considerations will persuade many to refuse participation in the possible and probable international conflicts which now threaten the peace of the world."[1] Transparently clear as the issue appears to our own people, we cannot be blind to the fact that on the side of our foes even Christian judgment sees the matter in a very different perspective. In spite of the Nazi persecution of the Church, there is no evidence whatever that Christian opinion in Germany does not stand solidly behind the national cause. In Italy "Christian" approval of the war is such that the Italian bishops are said to have petitioned Mussolini to extend the "crusade" to the Holy Land. No one sees more clearly than does Niebuhr himself the virtual impossibility, where war is the field of inquiry, of reaching a discriminate judgment unbiassed by purely national and selfish interests. As he says in his latest booklet, "No nation defends 'civilization' or 'truth' unless there is some coincidence between these values and its own national self-interest."[2] And when we allow such a judgment as to relative justice to become a motivating factor in determining our *religious* duty (as indeed every Christian non-pacifist is bound to do), the peril is obvious: "The political judgment that it is imperative to destroy the Nazi regime may be valid

[1] *An Interpretation of Christian Ethics*, 204.
[2] *Europe's Catastrophe and the Christian Faith*, 24 f.

enough. But we cannot raise such a political judgment to the emi-
nence of a religious judgment without falling prey to the errors and
illusions of Nazi religion. It is of the very essence of Nazi religion
to identify salvation with the defeat of one's foes. This is the most
primitive of all religions. It is a tribal religion . . ."[1] "It is not a good
thing to recommend the Christian faith as a source of morale in war
time."[2] Were there some international authority which could pro-
nounce unbiassed judgment as to which side was waging a relatively
"just war", then one could see more logic both in the Catholic
doctrine of a righteous defence and in Niebuhr's own brilliant
argumentation. But the tragic truth is that there is no such
authority, while the Church, which might have been one, has
almost invariably in its national branches blessed, on both sides, all
wars between "Christian" countries. We are not denying that
Niebuhr is right when he insists that we ought to use Jesus' ethics
as a principle of discriminate as well as of absolute judgment; we are
suggesting that in the case of war an unbiassed judgment is virtually
impossible, and the verdict is far too uncertain to justify recourse to
a method of "defence" which is admittedly utterly irreconcilable
with those very principles which are our canon of judgment.

(b) *Is War Ever the Lesser Evil?*

Secondly, it is argued that when submitted to our principle of
discriminate criticism war may be seen to be the less of two evils,
and therefore a legitimate activity for the Christian. The evil consequences of not using the war method would be greater than the
admitted evil consequences of using it. War is evil, but the results
of pacifism would be worse. Materially? Opinions will differ. Here
is Dean Inge, not of course a confessed pacifist: "The burden of
proof always lies with the nation which chooses war, and the reasons
alleged are generally, in part at least, hypocritical. That war is the
greatest evil in human life, and that no good can ever come of it, are
in my opinion certain. . . . When we consider that war between
civilized nations is condemned by common sense and humanity;
that it is a negation of the religion which most of us profess; that its
futility has been amply demonstrated; that, as Wellington said,
there is nothing worse than winning a war except losing it; that it
involves the sacrifice of our deepest affections and of the objects to
which our working lives are directed, must we not suspect that the
exalted motives by which we believe ourselves to be animated are a
rationalization of deep-seated instincts which have their roots in the
unconscious mind, and which, if they were realized for what they

[1] *Europe's Catastrophe and the Christian Faith*, 12.
[2] Ibid., 32.

are, might not receive the sanction either of our conscience or of our intelligence?"[1] Pacifists at least have the right to their conviction that, before peace returns, the hard logic of events will have proved that total war is a disaster immeasurably worse than any which a consistent pacifism could have involved. And, in any case, how far ought the estimate of probable material consequences to enter into the determination of Christian conduct? Ought a Christian to participate in an acknowledged evil in the hope of escaping from a hypothetically greater evil still? And if he believes that obedience to the way of Christ as he sees it will find its response in the release of the redemptive power of God transforming the whole situation, does not the estimation of material consequences become wellnigh impossible? And morally? Put the pacifist alternative to war at its worst: "All their political alternatives," says Niebuhr of pacifists, "finally reduce themselves to one, capitulation to tyranny."[2] Even so, which is the greater moral evil? Jesus did not wage the expected Messianic war: He did bid His disciples to submit to the exactions of the tyrant. We too often forget that the "Caesar", to whom Jesus commanded his dues to be rendered, was the dictator of a foreign power in occupation of His own home land.

But the alternative, war or capitulation to tyranny, is no true one. It becomes so only if, like Niebuhr, we first eliminate Jesus' own alternative. To this we return. Meantime it is apposite to ask: When war is chosen as the only apparent alternative to tyranny, is it ever the case, historically speaking, that the Law of Love, exercising its discriminating function, is the deciding factor in the choice? If so, just when is it that the Law of Love exercises its compulsion? Let an acute journalist answer: "The tacit reply of most military apologists is, 'When the Government declares war.' Unless Reinhold Niebuhr accepts the divine infallibility of his Foreign Office, how does he make his own decision? There is tyranny in Japan: is Niebuhr fighting it? There is tyranny in Germany, and was for many years before this war began: did Niebuhr urge war then? Where in the theology of Reinhold Niebuhr is there to be found the explanation of the immediate change brought about by the action of a 'relatively good' Government? In these matters of relativity the Government decides, and the moral philosopher is not consulted. ... For war is not humanly willed as a reluctant choice in opposition to tyranny among the relativities of political life; it is part of the current situation, as much a natural child of modern European society as tyranny itself. When Niebuhr chooses war, he does not, in reality, oppose tyranny; he allows himself to become an unresist-

[1] *The Fall of the Idols*, 185, 191 f.
[2] Article in *Life and Work*, December 1940.

ing member in a retrogressive process of which war and tyranny are equally a part."[1] Niebuhr complains that pacifists "are willing to grant a distinction between a democratic civilization and tyranny, but not enough of a distinction to act upon it."[2] To which the pacifist may justly reply that, as he deliberately stands back from the current, his act of decision is infinitely more real than that of the vast majority of those who go with the tide. British pacifists, quite apart from any considerations of conscience, might claim that they have judged their own institutions preferable to those of Germany, and have also judged that the methods of total war are more likely than not to replace the former by the latter: and they are acting accordingly. On the other hand, how many Christian non-pacifists of Niebuhr's complexion would feel bound to take up arms against their own country, if the Law of Love in its discriminating function should ever decide that the enemy had the juster cause?

(c) *Loyalty to Caesar or Loyalty to God?*

A final judgment of relative values is called for in the resolving of the conflict of loyalties by which every Christian is in war-time beset. How to reconcile the claims of Caesar with the claims of God? No Christian can escape the agony of the dilemma. He is bound up with the community of his fellow-citizens in all the relationships and responsibilities of ordinary life. He cannot contract out of these relationships except by renouncing life itself. If he refuses loyal co-operation in war he seems to be declining to play his part in defending a social structure whose protection and nurture he himself still needs and still accepts. The Christian who refuses military service cannot therefore be said to be doing the ideally right thing. But the truth is that, for one who sees war to be utterly irreconcilable with the will of God in Christ, once war has broken out there is no way for the time being of reconciling God's claim upon him through the duty he owes to his fellows with God's claim upon him through the voice of his own conscience. Both claims he cannot wholly satisfy, and either way he will confess that he has not wholly fulfilled the obligations of Christian citizenship. Yet surely here, if anywhere, we must dare a discriminate judgment. In face of the present tendency to absolutize state and nation and to exalt loyalty to the state to almost the same level as loyalty to God, the Christian must fearlessly confess that state and nation still belong to the sphere of earthly and relative values, and that God alone has claim to absolute and unconditional loyalty. "We are all members", writes Dean Inge, "of many societies or organizations, each of which has a limited and

[1] W. J. S. N. Grindlay in *Peace Commentary.*
[2] Article in *Life and Work*, December 1940.

indefeasible claim upon us. . . . Our highest duty in each of these spheres is summed up in our duty to God, that is to say, our homage to those absolute and eternal values in which the nature and will of the Deity are revealed to us. Some of these claims are narrower than the State, others still wider. What possible reason is there for singling out the State as the one all-embracing and absolute sovereign power?"[1] To one who sees in the words of Jesus the laws of a transcendent Kingdom given to be obeyed on earth, and sees in the Church Catholic and oecumenical the fellowship of the redeemed and the very Body of Christ the Redeemer, to such a one the obligation to maintain the unity and communion of that fellowship, even across the boundaries of warring states, may well seem to override every other loyalty; and participation in war, involving as it does the diabolical breaking of the Body yet again, may well seem an evil far more shameful than any failure in the duty of citizenship which may be involved in a refusal to uphold a national state by war. For such a judgment each of us must accept his own responsibility. We must have nothing but respect for the majority of Christians who, with equal sincerity, reach the opposite conclusion. Only God knows whether we or they are right. We can but say with St. Paul, "I know nothing against myself; (that is, I have nothing on my conscience) yet am I not hereby justified: but He that judgeth me is the Lord."[2]

[1] *The Fall of the Idols*, 132.
[2] I Cor. iv. 4.

CHAPTER SIX

THE CHRISTIAN ALTERNATIVE

JUDGED by the New Testament the greatest weakness of Niebuhr's case, the less excusable because it lies at the very central point of the Gospel, is his failure to give any adequate place to the distinctively Christian method of overcoming evil—the redemptive power of active, self-sacrificial love, which has its symbol in the Cross. Thus he charges pacifists that, when they are confronted by the duty of making the crucial discriminate judgment, "the ambiguity of all historical decisions persuades some Christians of perfectionist tendencies not to make a decision at all."[1] So might Jesus' Zealot critics have taunted Him when He rejected the war method and "steadfastly set His face to go to Jerusalem."[2] Did Jesus really make no decision at all when He chose the Cross? To Niebuhr pacifism is apparently "non-resistance" pure and simple, to stand passive before evil with folded hands. In truth its dominant note, so far as it claims to be Christian, is unceasing resistance to evil, but with weapons very different from those of war. And here the pacifist stands in the true Christian tradition: "What then", asks St. Chrysostom, "ought we not to resist an evil? Indeed we ought; but not by retaliation. Christ hath commanded us to give up ourselves to suffering wrongfully, for thus shall we prevail over evil. For one fire is not quenched by another fire, but fire by water."[3]

Non-resistance and Non-Retaliation

This is the authentic New Testament note. In spite of Niebuhr's argument under this head, the emphasis in the New Testament is much more on "non-retaliation" than on "non-resistance." Perhaps this is so even in the crucial "non-resistance" sayings of Matthew v. 38 ff. Some scholars consider that the logic of the passage demands "retaliate not upon evil" rather than "resist not evil", and that even the Greek suggests a possible mistranslation of the original Aramaic which may have run: "You have heard that it was said, An eye in return for an eye, and a tooth in return for a tooth. But I say unto you, Do not render evil in return for evil." The truest interpretation of the Master would then be St. Paul's words, "Render to no man evil for evil. . . . Be not overcome of evil, but overcome evil with

[1] Article in *Life and Work*, December 1940. [2] Luke ix. 51.
[3] *Nicene and Post Nicene Fathers*, X, 93.

good."[1] In any case Jesus' religion was always positive and not negative—"thou shalt love", not "thou shalt not fight." In the Sermon on the Mount the corollary to "resist not evil" is "do good to them that hate you." The negative injunction to non-resistance, falsely assumed by so many to represent the whole pacifist ethic, is immediately followed by the positive commandment of all-embracing love, yes, a love that includes even "enemies." And precisely here is the new element in Jesus' teaching: retributive justice, which merely checks and punishes evil, is supplanted by active, self-sacrificing love, which redeems and changes the evil will, so overcoming evil in the only way by which it can be truly overcome. And it is this great truth, not merely passive "non-resistance," which must always be the foundation of the pacifist position when it is adopted on specifically Christian grounds.

Love and Righteousness

The chief count in the charge of "heresy" brought by Niebuhr and others against Christian pacifism is that love is emphasized out of all proportion to righteousness, or justice, so that the whole Christian ethic becomes distorted. Now we are dealing here with two complementary qualities in the nature of God Himself, "Righteousness" and "Love." And according to the New Testament, as the expression of these qualities and their counterpart on the plane of human relationships, it may be said that we have the "Law" and the "Gospel"—the Law being the expression of God's Righteousness and the Gospel the expression of His Love.

Now in Christian thought there can be no real contradiction between "Righteousness" and "Love" on the one hand, nor between the "Law" and the "Gospel" on the other. Yet it must be admitted that there may be a consciously felt "tension" between Righteousness and Love, and between the Law and the Gospel respectively; and only by resolving this tension in the right way will disastrous errors of emphasis be avoided. The Christian pacifist believes—and here he would claim to be in line with the whole New Testament—that Love is "super"-Righteousness, or "transformed" Righteousness, or Righteousness "fulfilled," in the sense in which Jesus uses the word "fulfil" in the Sermon on the Mount. In the same way the Gospel is "super"-Law, or "transformed" Law, or Law "fulfilled." In this peculiar New Testament sense of the word, to "fulfil" something means to "fill it full", to "give its full content", to declare or to practise the whole of which that something is but the part. To "fulfil" Righteousness is to declare and to practise the

[1] Rom. xii. 14 ff.

Love of which Righteousness is but part; for Love in itself comprises all the other qualities of God; and to "fulfil" the Law is to proclaim and to practise the Gospel, of which the Law is but the imperfect foreshadowing. Thus Jesus by His way of life fulfils the Law by so completing it that it is transformed into the Gospel, and fulfils Righteousness by so completing it that it is transformed into Love.

Must the Law Precede the Gospel?

Here then is our reply to this charge of "heresy." The besetting sin of pacifism, we are told, is that it exalts the Gospel of Love at the expense of Justice and Law. Law, it is asserted, must always precede the Gospel; the enforcement of Law is the necessary preliminary to the appeal of the Gospel. Thus the Archbishop of York: "Sound doctrine and experience alike assure us that the stage of the Law must precede that of the Gospel, and that, though the Gospel carries us far beyond the law, we need the foundation provided by the Law to be secure before we can truly respond to the Gospel." All of which is largely true, and yet such a dangerous half-truth; and how easily it can be re-expressed in militarist terms! "Justice is the essential preliminary to peace; and Righteousness can/be established only on the foundation of universally acknowledged Law. Therefore let us by force of arms compel the observance of Law, and thereby vindicate the principle of Righteousness within which alone the Gospel can operate. Christ calls us to another war-crusade to end war."

But if it really be true that the Law must always precede the Gospel, then surely the whole argument of St. Paul's Epistles goes by the board. What inexcusable presumption to proclaim the Gospel to pagans without having first thoroughly disciplined them under the sanctions of the Law! Yet when St. Paul points to the faith of Abraham as an illustration that the "Promise" came first, and that the Law could not annul it,[1] he surely implies that Love is the essential quality in the Divine nature and the authentic spring of Divine action, while the way of Law is a second-best, "added because of transgressions", until the true way of Love could be finally and fully revealed in Christ. It is the very essence of New Testament teaching that the grace of God in the Gospel is operative towards men who are still unrighteous and not yet obedient to the Law's commands: "God commendeth His own love towards us, in that, *while we were yet sinners*, Christ died for us."[2] All the great Christian saints from St. Paul downwards have been reduced to despair precisely because they could not first obey the Law and

[1]Gal. iii. 15 ff.   [2]Rom. v. 8.

thereby "qualify" for the Gospel. If it is really the case that the foundation of Law has to be secure before we may present the Gospel and expect men to respond to it, then Christianity is after all a mere fair-weather religion, and its transforming ethic cannot function until it is no longer needed.

Love the "Fulfilment" of Justice

Niebuhr insists that, given a sinful world and the impracticability of the way of Love, our goal should be "equal justice", and that pacifists, with their pathetic confidence in the power of Love, betray the last chance of achieving it. But it is noteworthy that Jesus Himself insists that His new and distinctive Gospel-ethic, and in particular the definitely "pacifist" features in it, aim not at the "destruction" but at the "fulfilment" of that Law which is the very ground of any "equal justice." The whole section of the Sermon in question begins with the statement, "Think not that I came to destroy the Law or the prophets: I came not to destroy, but to fulfil."[1] And at the end of the section we have the "non-resistance" and the "love-your-enemy" sayings as the crowning illustration of what Jesus means by "fulfilling the Law." This in Jesus' thought evidently means to "give the full content" to the incomplete conception of Law, to draw out its underlying intention, to make explicit that which hitherto has been only implicit, to declare and to practise the whole Gospel of which the Law is but a part. Christians are guilty of "heresy", not when with Jesus and Paul we insist upon this transformation and "fulfilment" of the Law in the Gospel, but when with Marcion and some of his modern followers we set Justice and Love, the Law and the Gospel, in so sharp an antithesis as to suggest that, when we exalt the "fulfilled" whole, we thereby "destroy" the incomplete part. Jesus' teaching, as interpreted by Christian pacifism, does not mean that Righteousness is dethroned by Love. It does mean that all human relationships, like the relationship between God and man in Christ, must ultimately be based on Love; that Justice truly "fulfilled" is nothing less than Love, rather than Love a by-product of Justice; that if we aim at Love we shall establish Righteousness and Justice by the way; that we can in fact secure Niebuhr's "equal justice" only when we aim primarily not at it, but at the Love-relationship of which it is but an uncompleted part, yes, even if that quest demands the sacrifice of self to the uttermost.

The Way of the Cross

In the Cross this redemptive way of sacrificial love finds its

[1]Matt. v. 17.

perfect expression. It is Jesus' seal upon His assurance that man cannot cast out devils by the prince of devils, His witness to the weakness and folly of the sword, and to the triumphant power of the new way of overcoming evil with good. We err if we isolate the Cross as a unique divine transaction which has no bearing upon the ethic which Jesus taught or the way of life to which He called His disciples, having first trodden it Himself. For always it is not suffering as such that redeems, but the willingness to accept suffering rather than deny the truth, obedience to a particular way of life with self-sacrifice, if such should be God's will, as a possible crown. Not that this plumbs the depths of the mystery of the Cross. But at least we must see in it the inevitable climax, under the conditions which confronted Jesus, to a consistent life-practice of meeting evil, not by violence, but by the way of forgiving and reconciling love. The faith that this is the *only* Christian method of overcoming evil is not a mere appendage to the Gospel, but its very core and condition. If Jesus was wrong here, then He was wrong in the very crux of His message, and it is a mockery to call Him Lord. Jesus went to the Cross rather than betray that love-method; and in that sense every Christian may rightly and without presumption aspire to "imitate the Cross." It cannot be mere chance that no saying of Jesus is more often repeated in the Gospels than that in which He bids His disciples follow Him along the road of the Cross; and even if He was speaking only in metaphor, He could not have done so had He not seen in the way of life which He set before them something in common with His own supreme sacrifice. And words such as these of St. Peter show that His disciples did so understand Him: "For hereunto were ye called: because Christ also suffered for you, leaving you an example, that ye should follow His steps . . . who His own self bare our sins in His body upon the tree."[1]

The Challenge to the Church

During the war it became more and more evident each month that the non-pacifist, so far as he remained Christian, was being inexorably driven nearer and nearer to the pacifist position. Today there are multitudes of Christians who have hitherto rejected Christian pacifism but now acknowledge themselves to be "nuclear pacifists." For the truth is that the threat of nuclear warfare, by rendering obsolete the doctrine of the "just war" on which is based the orthodox belief that "it is lawful for Christians, at the commandment of the Magistrate, to wear weapons and serve in the wars" (XXXIX Articles; or, as the Westminster Confession has it:

[1] 1 Pet. ii. 21 ff.

"Christians may lawfully now under the New Testament wage war
upon just and necessary occasions."), has demonstrated beyond
argument that the theological foundations of the Christian non-
pacifist position have collapsed. Thus the British Council of
Churches declared (1946) that "it is clear that in so far as war
becomes total, in the sense that every means may be adopted that
appears conducive to victory, and that the attack is directed not
against armies but against nations by methods of mass destruction,
the restraints in waging war which have been regarded by the
Christian tradition as essential to a 'just' war disappear." The
World Council of Churches (1948) declared that "in these circumstances the tradition of a just war, requiring a just cause and the
use of just means, is now challenged." Finally in a document issued
by a Commission of the World Council (1958) under the title
"Christians and the Prevention of War in an Atomic Age" it is
acknowledged: "We maintain that none of the justifications used in
the past for a Christian participation in war can apply in the holo-
caust of total global war."

All these statements come from Christian non-pacifist sources,
and they suggest that unless (*per impossibile* !) the non-pacifist
position can be re-erected on a foundation other than that of the
doctrine of the "just war" the Church will be compelled, if only by
the logic of its own declarations, to adopt the full pacifist position.

What is the next step, and how can pacifist and non-pacifist best
work together for the prevention of war? It is urgent that we should
enlarge our common standing-ground. The World Council confessed at Amsterdam that "the Church appears impotent to deal
with the realities of the human situation because it has failed to
speak effectively on the subject of war." The effect of an unambiguous pronouncement by the whole Church (or even by one national
Church) on the question of war would be quite beyond calculation.
Professor Latourette, historian of the expansion of Christianity,
goes so far as to affirm: "There can be no reasonable question that
if the great majority of professed Christians, led by the Churches,
. . . were utterly and wholly to renounce war and decline to participate in it, were positively to do those things which make for peace,
reconciliation among the nations could be effected, peace become
the normal state of mankind, and international relations placed on
the basis of justice."[1] But short of accepting the pacifist position in
full, surely the time has come for the World Council to declare that
under no circumstances can the Church sanction nuclear warfare,
nor the manufacture and accumulation of nuclear weapons as an

[1] *The Church, the Gospel and War*, 110.

alleged deterrent against aggression. Can such "peace through fear" ever be anything but an obstacle to true and lasting peace?

Should war break out anew Christian pacifists will be confronted by the duty of making yet another "relative judgment." Taking a long view shall we best serve the cause of peace by abandoning our faith?—remembering, as Niebuhr himself has said, that "whether a man stands or yields in the hour of crisis is of course determined by commitments made before the crisis arises. Devotion to a cause may be such that it becomes irrevocable, and its revocation would result in the complete disintegration of personality."[1] Or shall we keep bright our witness to a better way?

[1] *An Interpretation of Christian Ethics*, 227.